PROTECTING YOUR BRAND

Todd M. Hess, Esq.
Intellectual Property Attorney
Certified Financial Planner®
Registered Professional Engineer

Wesley Chapel
Press

5922 Weddington Rd, Suite A5
Wesley Chapel, NC 28104

Permissions
Wesley Chapel Press
5922 Weddington Road, Suite A5
Wesley Chapel, NC 28104

Printed in the United States of America

2 3 4 5 6 7 8 9 0

ISBN No. 978-1-7333708-0-6

Table of Contents

Introduction

This book is intended to be a guide to those involved in developing brands to help them better understand the need for brand protection. Provided are overviews of the branding process from the trademark perspective. Chapter 1 provides an overview of the importance of brand recognition and the need for protection of the brand. Chapter 2 describes the types of marks that may be used in association with the brand to identify that brand and can be subject to registration in the United States Patent and Trademark Office ("USPTO").

Chapter 3 provides a somewhat comprehensive overview of international classifications of goods and services for registration of the associated marks. One or more of these classes—and it is typically more especially when used in association with a brand where a large number of products and/or services are provided—must be identified in association with the trademark or trademarks registered for that brand.

Chapter 4 describes the categories of marks and the variations in strength and weaknesses in these categories. This becomes particularly of importance if the validity of the mark ever comes into question. This is discussed more fully in Chapter 7, where likelihood of confusion is discussed, this being the main precipice in determining whether the trademark is infringed or not.

The two separate registers for registration of the trademark in the United States, and why one is good and the other is not so good in the protection of a mark is the subject of Chapter 5. Chapter 6 details the items needed in the application for registration of a trademark, how the mark should be identified prior to registration and the identified following registration in order to place competitors on notice concerning ownership of the mark.

Chapter 8 discusses survey evidence and the importance of properly identifying the universe of users your brand targets. Chapter 9 identifies the damages and monetary relief that may be available for infringement. This chapter establishes your value for the trademark in the protection of your brand, and the potential costs in the event you are found to infringe the trademark of another even if such infringement is unintentional. Finally, Chapter 10 identifies alternatives to litigation in the event there is more than one party that wants to use a similar mark in association with their brand.

While the book is largely intended for those involved with developing a brand and the protection of marks that are associated with the brand, the author apologizes in advance for including footnotes that reference supporting statutes and case law for some of the information provided in the book. These citations are typically of no concern to those professionals involved with building and maintaining a brand, they have been included in the event an attorney chooses to use the book in association with their own practice.

Please enjoy the book. There is also an online course available that is also offered at client's sites in the event you have an interest in ensuring your team is properly trained on these concepts. Please don't hesitate to reach out to the author if you need any assistance.

Sincerely,

Todd M. Hess, Esq.

CHAPTER 1: The Importance of Brand Recognition

It is a well-known premise that our brains respond differently to names over other words that are generally used but that lack any well-established association. Endorphins excite our brain when we hear the sound of a name with which we have established a positive recognition. Such a positive recognition may be the result of our own favorable experience associated with perhaps a stay at a hotel having a distinctive brand name, when dining at a restaurant having a brand name characteristic of the eating place where you had an enjoyable dining experience, or a positive and memorable use of a product having a unique brand name. Of course, a brand name associated with any of these services or products becomes a moniker through which others may recommend such services or products establishing the needed response in a person's mind when seeing or recollecting a past referral. For example, the following brand names typically establish a positive experience in the minds of most persons relative to the generic product name:

CINNEBON® versus Cinnamon Roll
STARBUCKS® versus Coffee
TOBLERON® versus Candy Bar
NATHAN'S® versus Hot Dog
BUDWEISER® versus Beer

However, names with which we have established negative associations can induce negative reactions as well. For example,

CopyCAT knock-off fragrances (United Kingdom)
YOU'RE FIRED trademark to Donald Trump

SARAH PALIN
NEW COKE renamed COKE II discontinued in 2002

While no one brand may appeal to everybody, the goal of the branding effort is to appeal to those who are likely to buy your product or to engage in your services. Thus, the marketing effort in developing the brand may initially be more focused, but it can be expanded to include other products and/or services if the brand is found to appeal to others.

Conventionally, marketing was focused upon selling, but now marketing is primarily focused upon branding. Money and time focused on branding can continue to produce benefits for the organization whereas when the primary focus is upon selling, the brand may not experience the needed growth.

Selling is actually in decline, because customers are more in the mode of buying. The Internet has become the dominant platform in terms of searching for needed products and services. Customers know what they are looking for and generally include those requirements in a search. If the product or service does not match the criteria that they are looking for, then it gets bypassed. However, when a customer recognizes a brand that they have developed a positive experience with, the endorphins drive the customer to further exploring that brand to see if it meets the criteria, and even if it does not fully meet that criteria, the customer may gain a recognition of why a certain criteria is not of any importance given the positioning of the brand in the marketplace.

To further demonstrate that this has become a buyer's market driven by the Internet that is supported by branding, the behemoth Internet products seller Amazon offers independent merchants that sell on its website marketing support, product reviews and prominent display, but, in exchange, Amazon acquires the right to purchase these

merchants brand name. The purchase is for a fixed price, and typically amounts to $10,000. Such a strategy allows Amazon to build more exclusive brands for its selling platform. However, the company is under scrutiny for anticompetitive practices, and it is uncertain whether such practices will be targeted in the future.

The Internet has clearly changed the way that products and services are branded. For example, travel agents used to book travel arrangements for people. However, now, with the Internet people are able to search out the fare they are willing to pay. In some cases, depending on the provider of those services and that person's experience with the provider, they may be driven to pay a little higher price to become comfortable with those services. Travel is just one example where people now digitally seek out their product and service choices. The Internet is a catalyst for the move from a seller's market to a buyer's market.

While there have been big brand successes on the Internet—for example Amazon.com, Google.com, etc.—this does not necessarily mean your company or organization needs to have a similar branding effort on the Internet. For example, Apple has not only been successful at selling online, but also accommodates sales through its app as well as through its Apple Stores. Indeed, many goods and services are still amenable to having a bricks and mortar store for the customer to stop with questions or to define the fine product form or service or even to obtain service on a previously purchased product they may be seeking out. An analysis of the extent of involvement your company or organization has on the Internet should be done in tandem with the branding strategy.

Not only expansion of a brand on the Internet, but any expansion of the brand whatsoever, leads to the concern and possibility of diluting the impact the brand has on those products and/or services added to the brand's scope. Examples of this dilution in the past have included certain automobile manufacturers including Chevrolet, for example, and, even to some extent, Tesla who has expanded the reach of its name beyond a myriad of electric cars, but also extends to an electric boat, supercharger stations to power these transportation devices and "clean" power-based tools including solar panels.

When marketing and brand building become inextricably linked, marketing becomes a component of the brand building process. However, brand building constitutes other components including product or service quality control, reliable product delivery, responsive customer service—*i.e.*, those sides of the organization that the customer typically see or have some connection with. In essence, a brand is a commitment to the buyer that the product or experience they are purchasing drives the desired feeling they achieve when it is used. This confluence of economics and the psychological impact drives the existence of brands.

In addition to the factors identified above, legal use and protection of the mark associated with a brand is another component of the brand building and preservation process. Protection of the brand to prevent another party's inappropriate use of the marks in association with the brand is the subject of trademark law. Furthermore, ensuring the use of a mark in association with the brand does not infringe upon the intellectual property rights of others, which could prove costly to the brand. The legal protections of marks associated with the brand and any markss that may be in conflict with those in use in association with the brand is the subject-matter further explained in this book.

Businesses that strive to excel in some way through the services or products they offer, can miss a valuable opportunity to associate and continuously use a name connected with such services or products. Brands that are well-established allow a business' goods or services to be recognized in a

crowded market space where consumers have a lot of choices to select from.

From a legal standpoint, such marks may be registered with the United States Patent and Trademark Office ("USPTO") and become a registered trademark that is available for your sole use in connection with the service and/or product for which you have registered the mark. While there are common law rights in a mark that has not been registered, marks subject to common law protection have a much more limited scope of protection including protection only in the geographic area where the mark has been used in association with products and/or services. Also, if somebody else has registered that same mark in association with a service or product that resembles your service or product and predates your use, they can legally force you to stop using that mark. So, what typically amounts to less than a couple of thousand dollars in legal fees and registration costs to have a mark registered in the USPTO, usually is money well-spent in establishing and protecting a mark through which you can market your services or products without fear of retribution from others who may claim ownership to that mark.

Products and services typically have limited life cycles relative to the brand used to promote them. Brands can continue to survive even when products or services that they are used in association with terminate and become replaced by upgraded or revised products or services. Brands may continue to be used to convey quality, credibility and experience in replacement products and/or services. Brands and associated marks add value to a company and can be found on the balance sheet of many of these companies. Also, the brands and associated trademarks of a company that is being considered for purchase should be evaluated as part of the due diligence process in establishing the value of the company.

Many acquisitions of companies are motivated by the brands and associated marks in use that are being acquired. While these are considered intangible assets, they nonetheless represent a company's valuation. Some well-known examples include Tata

Motors of India's purchase of Jaguar and Range Rover from Ford for $2.56 billion; InBev's acquisition of Budweiser to continue to expand their worldwide distribution of brands that include Stella Artois (Belgium), Becks (Germany), Boddingtons (United Kingdom), SABMiller (acquired afterwards) and Tolstiak (Russia) Labatt; and Kraft's purchase of Cadbury for $19.5 billion and then later H.J. Heinz Co.'s purchase of Kraft Foods as supported by Warren Buffett at close to $37 billion. Interestingly, Kraft-Heinz eventually took a goodwill impairment charge and wrote down the value of Kraft and Oscar Meyer brands by $15.4 billion, apparently demonstrating that certain brands may be accredited with too much value upon acquisition.

In addition to brand strength that already has been established, some marks may be of importance due to the creative aspects of the companies with which they are associated. In particular, established trademarks in hotel and restaurants tend to encompass the creative aspects of accommodations or the preparation and presentation of dining fair. Some examples of registered trademarks used in association with hotels and/or restaurants include YOUR MOM'S HOUSE®, SEA WATCH® and BEACH HUT®, which are examples of word marks. Designs or a design plus words may also be registered, with the latter being more preferred when attempting to establish some needed name recognition.

If you have a business and you want to establish or you have established a positive experience surrounding a particular mark, then you should consider registering that mark as a trademark to safeguard the marketing protection you have in association with that mark. Brand protections also add value to a business.

Logos as Brands

A logo is a graphical design representing a company or a brand. A design may be generally classified according to three types: logomark, logotype and combination mark.

Logomark

A logomark is an image or design that represents a company or a brand, but typically does not include the name of the company with which the image or design is associated. For example, the Pepsi Globe, as illustrated here, is a red, white and blue design in a sphere-like shape often characterized as encompassing a "smile." The Pepsi Globe likely represents one of the world's most recognized logomarks. If a company is successful at branding around a highly successful logomark, then the mark itself establishes great range and generates a strong visual identify for the company. Pepsi, for example, uses this established mark in association with its Pepsi products. For example, Pepsi or PepsiCo, Inc. has registered the mark in the United States in International Class 025 in association with hats, sweatshirts and t-shirts (*see*, *e.g.*, U.S. Registration No. 3,729,649 registered on December 22, 2009), and International Class 032 in association with concentrates, syrups or powders used in the preparation of soft drinks and soft drinks themselves (*see*, *e.g.*, U.S. Registration No. 3,670,829 registered August 18, 2009). (International classes are discussed in more detail in Chapter 3.)

Upon adopting a revised design for the Pepsi globe, the company allowed the designs that were held pending the decision on which of the final designs to adopt to become cancelled or abandoned. These former designs (often represented in black & white in the USPTO to obtain the most expansive coverage) included the following:

Clearly, Pepsi has a well-established plan in place to protect any of the marks that it may choose to eventually adopt in the end after gauging preferred customer acceptance of the brand.

<u>Logotype</u>

A logotype is a word mark but in stylized logo form. While this approach leaves the designer with limited creative scope, the logotype mark is usually the most preferred approach upon adoption of a logo mark, since it immediately associates the business name with the brand. *I.e.*, the more literal the illustration in the logotype, the less work with respect to association of the logo to the brand that eventually needs to be established. Due to the creative limitations placed upon the design, the logotype may not be the preferred image for creative businesses or hospitality industries seeking to draw customers due to creative aspects of the business through the design. However, Google or Alphabet, Inc. has become quite creative in adapting the Google name on its web page to coincide with events of the day.

<u>Combination Mark</u>

The combination mark combines both a logomark and a logotype expanding the creative freedom to allow the mark to almost become immediately positioned to represent the brand or brands of the company. There are integrated combination marks allowing both text and the image to become representative of the brand, and standalone combination marks that includes a separate logomark and logotype. The following table and associated images provides representations of various combination marks that have been adopted by businesses many of which you are probably already familiar with:

1 Registered trademark of Federal Express Corporation.
2 Registered trademark of AT&T Intellectual Property, Inc.
3 Registered trademark of Hershey Chocolate & Confectionery Corporation.
4 Registered trademark of TripAdvisor LLC.
5 Registered trademark of Frito Lay North America, Inc.

6 Registered trademark of Goodwill Industries International Inc.
7 Registered trademark of Oldemark LLC.
8 Registered trademark of Apple Inc.
9 Registered trademark of Boston Beer Corporation.
10 Registered trademark of HUGO BOSS Trade Mark Management GmbH & Co.
11 Registered trademark of McDonald’s Corporation.
12 Registered trademark of NBCUniversal Media, LLC.
13 Registered trademark of SSE IP, LLC.
14 Registered trademark of United States Postal Service.
15 Registered trademark of Microsoft Corporation.
16 Registered trademark of Marriott International, Inc.
17 Registered trademark of Disney Enterprises, Inc.
18 Registered trademark of Disney Enterprises, Inc.
19 Registered trademark of The Coca-Cola Company.
20 Registered trademark of Bayerische Motoren Werke Aktiengesellschaft.
21 Registered trademark of Chick-fil-A, Inc.
22 Trademark in the United States.
23 Registered trademark of American Automobile Association, Inc.
24 Registered trademark of Nike, Inc.
25 Registered trademark of American Family Life Assurance Company of Columbus.
26 Registered trademark of Levi Strauss & Co.

Branding in an organization requires much more than a logo, however. An organization's brand identity is primarily established by the investment the organization makes in its brand and the good will established in the goods and/or services associated with the brand. The logo is merely a pictorial illustration associated with the organization's brand allowing the organization's consumer base to recognize that organization's association with the brand. Certainly, it is most beneficial to the organization if the consumer recognition is positive. This response may only be achieved through the organization's commitment to deliver goods or services that are used in association with the brand in such a way that achieves this consumer recognition. Thus, the logo becomes a pictorial association of the brand image developed to draw the consumer's mindset to focus on the goods or services that are delivered using the brand

<u>Illustrative Logos</u>

Illustrative logos may be designed to cover a range of meanings. Some may be illustrative of the products and/or services being delivered under the brand name. Similar to literal elements that add identity to a logo, illustrations can embody, in some way, the type of goods or services that are provided under the brand to help to more immediately establish that brand recognition. *E.g.*, the following illustrations may be useful according to the corresponding type of organization:

	in association with dog grooming
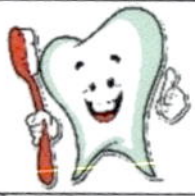	in association with a dentist
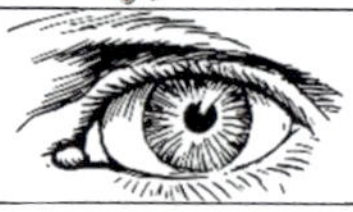	in association with optical care
	in association with the craft beer industry

	in association with relaxation and leisure
	in association with engineering services
	in association with information technology services
	in association with automobile service

As in the latter exampel, the image may be concrete, but the meaning that is conveyed is abstract. For example, your automobile needs service or it will resemble the image of the car in the logo. Likely, the most famous image with an abstract conveyance is the logo adopted by Apple having the styled image of an apple with a bite taken out of it. The designer of the Apple logo has clearly indicated that the bite out of the apple logo was merely intended to provide scale demonstrating the piece of fruit represented by the logo is an apple and not some other piece of fruit. Clearly, Apple does not sell apples that are grown from trees, but the image has become quite notorious in representing the Apple brand. The current logo was a replacement for the company's original logo where Isaac Newton was sitting under an apple tree.

Statutory Authority

The United States Constitution grants to Congress plenary authority over patents and copyrights whereby Congress has power "To promote the progress of science and useful arts, by securing for limited times to authors and inventors the exclusive right to their respective writings and discoveries." However, the United States Constitution is expressly silent with respect to the power to regulate trademarks or brand names. Rather, Congress

uses its authority under the Commerce Clause for the adoption of statutes under the Lanham Act for a national system of trademark registration and protections for the owner of a federally registered mark against the use of similar marks if such use is likely to result in consumer confusion, or if the dilution of a famous mark is likely to occur. Inasmuch, for trademarks to receive federal registration, they must be in "use in commerce."

The Lanham Act also allows an applicant to apply for registration of a mark if the applicant has a "bona fide intent" to use the mark in commerce, but registration will ultimately not be allowed until the applicant demonstrates that the mark is in actual use in commerce. Indeed, the failure to demonstrate such use or even to continue such use in commerce will cause the trademark neither to be granted or to become abandoned.

Court Precedent

A precedent is a legal case that establishes a principle or rule that is typically followed within the jurisdiction where the principle or rule has been determined. For example, there are 94 federal judicial courts that are divided among 12 regional circuits that each have their own appellate court. Precedent set by those appellate courts will apply to each of the district courts that are part of the associated district.

The United States Supreme Court established precedent that must be followed nationwide. In fact, many issues can be handled in the 12 circuit courts differently because the Supreme Court has not yet established a precedent. One example, is the determination of likelihood of confusion, as further discussed in Chapter 7.

Pursuant to the checks and balance system under the United States Constitution, the United States Supreme Court may determine whether the authority Congress has granted is itself constitutional. The Supreme Court has used this power in some more recent court cases whereby the Court has determined that certain provisions of the Lanham Act are not constitutional and may not be enforced. This, in particular, will be a discussion in Chapter 4 concerning whether certain types of marks can be subjected to trademark protection or not.

In certain opinions, the Supreme Court has weighed in concerning the use of trademarks and their nature for protecting an established brand. More recently, the Supreme Court has emphasized that the disparagement clause of the Lanham Act, which was intended by Congress to deny registration of marks that could be deemed to "disparage" any "person[], living or dead," is unconstitutional for the reason that it violates the Free Speech Clause of the First Amendment.[1] The Court rationalized whether the disparagement clause should be subjected to a lower level of scrutiny since trademarks are the subject of commercial speech. However, the Court rejected this notion arguing that the public expression of ideas may not be prohibited merely because the ideas themselves are offensive to some of the hearers.[2] Therefore, according to the Supreme Court, an organization may use a trademark to discriminate at will, but I am sure the Court recognizes that it is not prudent for an organization to do so when attempting to establish an accepted brand recognition for products or services used in association with such marks. Even more recently, in *Iancu*, the Supreme Court determined that the statute in the Lanham Act denying registration of an "immoral or scandalous" trademark is overly broad and also violates the First Amendment.[3] In this case, the Respondent attempted to register the trademark FUCT in association with a clothing line. Thus, the

---

[1] *Matal v. Tam*, 582 U. S. ____, 137 S. Ct. 1744, 1765, 198 L.Ed.2d 366 (2017).
[2] *Id.* at 1763 (*citing Street v. New York*, 394 U.S. 576, 592, 89 S.Ct. 1354, 22 L.Ed.2d 572 (1969)).
[3] *Iancu v. Brunetti*, No 18-302 (2019)

Supreme Court confirmed that the government cannot be meddling with an organization's use of an established brand regardless of how others may view the mark that is in use in association with that brand.

In addition to the Supreme Court, there are various other lower court decisions that have been definitive with respect to the use of the trademarks for brand protection. For example, appellate courts have found that product specific characteristics themselves constitute a commercial brand that is worth protecting. *Direct Niche, LLC v. Via Varejo S/A*, 898 F.3d 1144 (11th Ci., 2018) (trademarks in association with retail store names; *Pantone, Inc. v. Esselte Letraset, Ltd.*, 878 F.2d 601 (2nd Cir 1989) (trademark used in association with commercial artist supplies); *Hanson v. Triangle Publications*, 163 F.2d 74 (8th Cir., 1947) (trademark used in association with a monthly magazine directed to the interests of teenage girls); *Virtual Works v. Volkswagen of Am.*, 238 F.3d 264 (4th Cir., 2000) (inappropriate use of the trademark of an automobile manufacturer in a domain name); *John Deere and Co. v. Payless Cashways, Inc.*, 681 F.2d 520 (8th Cir., 1982) (trademark used in association with retail building materials store services); *Brandir Intern., Inc. v. Cascade Pacific Lumber Co.*, 834 F.2d 1142 (2nd Cir., 1987) (trademark used in association with a bicycle rack); *Schlafly v. Saint Louis Brewery, LLC*, 909 F.3d 420 (Fed. Cir., 2018) (trademark used in association with various types of beer); *Procter & Gamble Co. v. JL Prescott Co.*, 102 F.2d 773 (3rd Cir., 1939) (trademark used in association with a cleanser and powdered soap); *Cadbury Beverages, Inc. v. Cott Corp.*, 73 F.3d 474 (2nd Cir., 1996) (trademark used in association with drinks); *Parks LLC v. Tyson Foods, Inc.*, 863 F.3d 220 (3rd Cir., 2017) (trademark used in association with a sausage); *Conopco, Inc. v. May Dept. Stores Co.*, 46 F.3d 1556, 32 USPQ2d 1225 (Fed. Cir., 1994) (trademarks used in association with personal care products); *Carvel Corp. v. Noonan*, 350 F.3d 6 (2nd Cir., 2003) (trademark used in association with ice cream products). In reality, the list goes on and on.

Mark Selection

Recognizing the legal issues surrounding the protection of a mark used in association with an organization's brand is sometimes the antithesis of the strategy of those in marketing who are ready to promote a brand, gaining an understanding of any legal risks involved with respect to the protection of a mark is important in the prevention of unnecessary expenses that could be incurred in promoting a mark when that may eventually need to be undone. Even worse, a finding that the mark places the organization at risk of litigation for infringement due to likelihood of confusion with another well-established mark, is well worth an analysis before actively pursuing use of the mark.

There are several recommended steps in association with establishing the name, logo or other distinctive characteristic that is to be used in association with a branding activity. The choice of which mark to select or even whether to establish a brand name at all should involve six steps of analyses. First, a determination of whether there is any value whatsoever in adopting a mark or logo to be used in association with a branding strategy is needed. If the intended product or service is to be used in association with only one customer or a few customers, for instance, then there may be no justification in establishing a brand for further marketing. In contrast, however, many times a decision must be made concerning the viability of establishing a brand and associated mark, even though the product or service is to have a limited distribution at first. If the latter is expected, then many times it is worth seeking registration of the associated mark for future protection of that mark. The cost in association for applying for registration of a mark and achieving registration of that mark is relatively low in relation to the protection that is provided for continued use of the mark in the event the branding program does eventually develop to a significant degree.

If a decision is eventually made concerning the need to pursue a branding strategy, the next step of the analyses is for a team in the organization that understands the need for the development of the brand for the product or service to brainstorm and develop a list of potential marks that could be used in association with the brand. If the marks are to include an illustrative aspect, then a designer should also be involved that can develop a draft image of any illustrations that are contemplated being adopted as a part of any of the selected marks. Preferably, at least about five but preferably up to ten variations in marks should be identified that could be used in association with the brand. Such variations should include literal differences in the marks, and, if an illustrative aspect is considered, variations in the images as well.

The brainstorming team should also identify a list of potential jurisdictions where they may like the mark to receive protection. Trademark registrations are generally on a per country basis, but with an opportunity to reserve ultimate protection in certain countries on a reduced fee basis. Nonetheless, the countries of interest should be identified allowing for the possibility of and any obstacles for registration in those countries to be identified.

After the potential list of marks to be considered for adoption has been developed, then the third step is the legal evaluation of the strength versus weaknesses of these marks and whether the ultimate registration of any mark could be delayed or denied altogether for various statutory reasons under the Lanham Act, for example. The reasons for delay or denial of the registration are further discussed in Chapters 4 and 5. Based upon this analysis, the three strongest marks should be identified. After the selection team confirms that further analysis of the three selected marks should continue or if one or more of these marks should be replaced by any of the other marks identified on the initial listing, then the analysis of this condensed list of marks should proceed under the fourth step.

The fourth step involves, searches and identification of any registered or common law marks that could otherwise prevent the registration and unfettered use of the mark in association with the goods and/or services with which the mark will be associated. This analysis should be for each of the countries or jurisdictions that have been identified to eventually be of importance with respect to the brand strategy. Search results identified to be either identical or similar to the three marks in question will be categorized. Under this analysis, a likelihood of confusion of any identified conflicting marks should be conducted to determine whether any of the marks could be prevented from being registered at all, causing an opposition to be raised upon receipt of a notice of allowance or whether an infringement action could eventually be raised. The results of these analyses are reviewed and the likelihood whether any of the marks could eventually be registered is concluded. If registration is possible, a ranking of the top three marks from this analysis is identified based upon the likelihood that they could eventually be registered balanced against the risks that could prevent registration that have been identified.

The fifth step, which is sometimes ignored, is to collect customer acceptance concerning which of the top three marks identified in the fourth step would be preferred in association with the brand. It is very important that these customers understand the brands of interest and the use of the marks in association with that brand including prototypes of how the goods would be marked as well as any advertising or website use of the marks in promoting the brand.

The sixth step involves reviewing the results of the step four analysis as well as the step five analysis, if conducted, with the organizational team responsible for the brand, and a decision is made concerning which mark to proceed with for an application for registration. In the United States, the application for registration is typically filed with the USPTO. Many other countries/regional offices are Paris Convention countries that will allow a six-month timeframe from the application for registration in the United States to file and receive the priority date when the application was filed here. If countries of interest concerning where to use the mark are not Paris Convention countries, then a decision must be made to determine whether an application for registration should be filed in these countries at the same time the application is filed in the United States.

An alternative to proceeding with registration in the other countries after the application for registration in the United States is to file for registration under the Madrid Protocol. This system allows a mark to eventually be registered in a large number of countries by obtaining an international registration in those designated contracting states under the Madrid Protocol. While there is a fee for designating the countries of interest under the Madrid Protocol, this fee is substantially less than the fee required to proceed directly with an application for registration in the corresponding member country. The registration may be made effective in any of the designation member countries by paying the fees for the application for registration of the trademark in that country. If the organization eventually decides not to proceed with registration of the mark in some or even any of the designated member countries, then the fee for having the marks in this "holding pattern" is substantially less than it would have cost to directly file the application for registration in the member countries under the Madrid Protocol. Again, not all countries/regional offices subscribe to the Madrid Protocol, and an analysis and decision must be made on whether an application for registration of the trademark in these countries should be immediately pursued.

CHAPTER 2: A Trademark is not only a Name

Definition of Trademark and Service Mark

A trademark is not only a name, but the Trademark Act of 1946, as amended, (typically referred to herein as the "Lanham Act"), which is the federal statute that governs trademarks, defines that the term "trademark" includes any word, name, symbol or device or any combination thereof to identify and distinguish goods, including a unique product, from those manufactured or sold by others, and to indicate the source of the goods, even if that source is unknown.[1]

Similarly, this statute defines that a "service mark" includes any word, name, symbol or device or any combination thereof to identify and distinguish services, including a unique service, from the services of others and to indicate the source of the services, even if that source is unknown. While we distinguish between trademark and service mark in the definitions as provided here, throughout the remainder of this book, we will generally classify both of these types of marks simply as trademarks with the goods and/or services with which they are associated distinguished by the associated classes as further detailed in Chapter 3.

The Lanham Act further provides that, to become registered, the trademark must be in actual use at the time the application for registration of trademark is filed or the applicant must have a "bona fide" intention to use the trademark in commerce.[2] While Congress is given plenary or complete authority in Article I, Section 8 of the United States Constitution "to promote the Progress of Science and useful Arts, by securing for limited Times to Authors and Inventors the exclusive Right to their respective Writings and Discoveries" (*i.e.*, copyrights and patents), Congress is not given plenary authority to promote brands. Rather,

---

[1] 15 USC § 1127.

[2] 15 USC § 1051.

Congress used as a basis for adopting the Lanham Act their authority under the Commerce Clause whereby Congress is authorized to regulate commerce occurring between the States. Thus, for a mark to ultimately be registered, it must be shown that the mark is used in commerce or eventually is shown that the mark is used in commerce. Additionally, for a trademark to remain registered in the USPTO, the mark must continue to be used in commerce or else the mark will be considered to have become abandoned.

Word Marks

Examples of trademarks that are either a word or a combination words include AMAZON®, EXXON® and YOU'RE FIRED!™. Note that the latter mark also includes punctuation as part of the trademark as well, which is also allowed, although punctuation is not considered to considerably alter the commercial impression of the mark.

Slogans are a combination of words and function as a trademark if the slogan identifies and distinguishes the goods and services of the company that uses the slogan over the goods and services of others. However, slogans cannot receive trademark protection if the slogan does not create a commercial impression that is distinct from the other material on the label or webpage in which it is used; the slogan provides explanation, instructions or other information that is not of a commercial nature; the slogan is commonly found in use in the industry not providing a distinctive characteristic of the company using the slogan; and the slogan merely conveys an advertising message. Exemplary slogans that have received trademark protection include MADE ITS WAY BY THE WAY IT'S MADE®; QUALITY MEANS SAFETY, AND SAFETY MEANS EVERYTHING®; PRECISE ON-TIME WORK EXCEEDING REQUIREMENTS® and DEDICATED TO THE RELENTLESS PURSUIT OF UPTIME®.

Slogans that are deemed descriptive in nature may be protected upon a showing of acquired distinctiveness or secondary meaning (described in more detail in Chapter 4).

<u>Design Marks</u>

The concept of design marks or logos has already been introduced in Chapter 1. An application to register a mark having a design element must include a special form drawing showing the mark in black on a white background unless the mark includes a claim to color. If a trademark has design elements, the USPTO has design codes that identify the prominent elements found in the design mark. Identification of these codes would allow the Trademark Electronic Search System ("TESS") to be searched to determine if any marks have these same prominent elements. It may then be determined whether any currently registered design marks could be confusingly similar to the mark that you would like to register. (The elements associated with likelihood of confusion or a confusingly similar mark analysis are discussed in Chapter 7.)

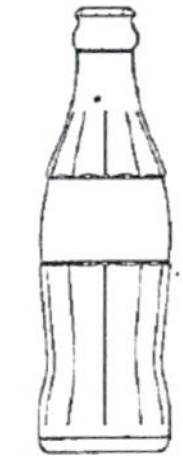

By way of example, the illustrated mark including the elephant shown here (registration no 5,747,554 used in association with retail store services) has the prominent features of an elephant having design code 03.03.01, a stylized elephant having design code 03.03.24 and a flag or pennant having design code 24.09.02. Searching TESS using these codes identifies the following marks having similar design elements that, for a multiple number of reasons, would probably not be considered confusingly similar to the above mark:

Symbols

A symbol is representative of a mark having a representative element in stylized logo form. The McDonald's logo is representative of a symbol, for example, otherwise known as the golden arches which is a stylized letter "M". The arches were part of the original restaurant design, but the company has moved away from that. While it is reported that in the 1960's McDonald's was prepared to abandon the mark, the mark's designer Louis Cheskin successfully urged the company to maintain this branding with its Freudian symbolism of a pair of nourishing breasts.

Graphic Marks

Examples of graphic marks include the following Apple and Pepsi logos as earlier discussed in Chapter 1.

However, graphics may be as simple as line drawings or drawings representative of some other image as further illustrated here.

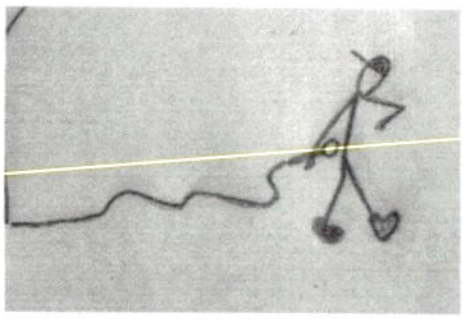

Indeed, design code 02.01.33 is representative of "grotesque men formed by letters, numbers, punctuation or geometric shapes" and "stick figures," and is relatively frequently used by the USPTO for design marks.

Logos

Following from graphics are logos, which include a graphic representation or design and also includes words, letters and/or numbers. The Starbucks logo is one notable example. However, through their abundance of graphical promotion, Google has established the number "1" having its typical signature colors of "yellow, red, blue and green" that is used in association with its mobile application for managing and accessing subscription-based services offering storage of electronic media.

Color Marks

The Supreme Court has ruled that color alone may be registered as a trademark under the Lanham Act.[3] However, in order to be eligible to be registered as a trademark, the color must have attained "secondary meaning" whereby the color identifies and distinguishes a particular brand thus indicating the source of the provided goods. Secondary meaning will be discussed in more detail later in Chapter 4.

The *Qualitex* case involved a shade of green-gold used in association with dry cleaning press pads. The following provides other examples of colors that have been registered as trademarks and an indication of the products the color is used in association with.

Color	Description	Registrant	Serial No.
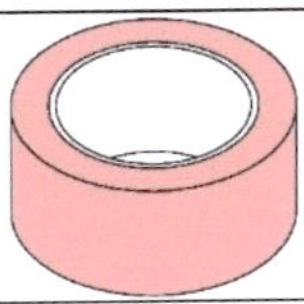	Color pink as applied to adhesive tape in its entirety.	Owens-Corning Fiberglass, Inc.	78,724,143

[3] *Qualitex Co. v. Jacobson Products Co.*, 514 U.S. 159, 115 S.Ct. 1300, 131 L.Ed.2d 248, 34 USPQ2d 1161 (1995).

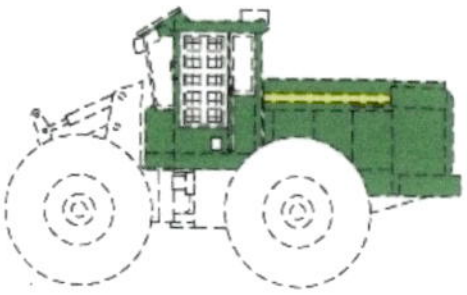	Combination of green and yellow where green is applied to an exterior surface of the machine and a yellow stripe is applied to a portion of exterior surface.	Deere & Company	85,404,464
	Canary yellow used over the entire surface of stationary notes.	3M Company	75,087,575
	Color brown applied to the vehicles used in performing transportation and delivery of personal property services.	United Parcel Service of America, Inc.	75,039,323

Aromas or Scents

While the USPTO allows registration of an aroma or a scent, there have not been many applications for registration of these types of "marks." For example, Hasbro, Inc. registered "a scent of sweet, slightly musky, vanilla fragrance, with slight overtones of cherry, combined with the smell of a salted, wheat-based dough" (registration no. 5,467,089) used in association with toy modeling products and, presumably, a scent found in its Play-Doh product line.

Verizon has registered the "flowery musk scent" (registration no. 4,618,936) that commonly can be found in its retail stores. Grendene S.A. has registered the scent of bubble gum used in association with its shoes, sandals and flip-flops (registration no. 4,754,435).

The requirement for registering a scent with the USPTO is that the only important practical function of the scent is to identify and distinguish the brand with which the scent is in use. Therefore, scents for perfumes or air fresheners cannot be registered as trademarks.[4]

Sound Marks

The USPTO also allows registration of sounds that distinguish the goods and/or services and indicate the source of the goods and/or services. While the MGM lion is likely the most notorious of sounds that have been registered, other sounds that more specifically define the sound have been registered as well. For example, the sound under registration no. 5,784,654 is described to be a "vibraphone playing the melody and harmony" where the "melody consists of 4/4 time signature, 4 beats, with notes D4, B4, D4 as triplet in beat 1, E4, C4, F4 triplet in beat2, with half note G4 in beats 3 and 4" and the "harmony consists of a quarter D4, followed by a quarter G4, followed by a half note chord of D4 and G4 together." Indeed, the description of many sounds is found in this type of form.

Figure or Number Marks

Figures or numbers may also be registered if it can be demonstrated that the figure or number identifies and distinguishes a particular brand and serves to indicate the source of the associated goods and/or services. Most figures or numbers tend to also include a design element (see Google's number 1 mark illustrated earlier in this Chapter). For example, the number "420" has been registered based upon its use in association with energy drinks, and "4711," originally registered in 1905, remains active and used in association with cologne water.

Number Marks

Numbers are strong trademarks when they do not have recognizable descriptive meaning. However, numbers are considered descriptive when they are recognizable abbreviations for descriptive terms. It was argued that the 7-Eleven store name was descriptive of the stores opening times from 7:00 am to 11:00

---

4 *See, e.g.*, *Calvin Klein Cosmetics Corp. v. Lenox Laboratories, Inc.*, 815 F.2d 500, 503 (8th Cir., 1987) (the legal relevance of a trademark is to show the source, identity, sponsorship, or origin of the product).

pm but became protectable upon establishing secondary meaning. Similarly, numbers are descriptive if they are an indicator of size, model, style or grade, but can be protectable upon establishing secondary meaning. (Chapter 4 goes through the concept of establishing secondary meaning in a mark that otherwise allows the mark to be subject to trademark protection.)

Letter Marks

Similar to numbers, as discussed above, letters may also individually be registered but typically include the letter in combination with some design element. Again, akin to its number "1", Google has demonstrated its branding prowess by doing the same with the use of the letter "G" in combination with its signature "yellow, red, blue and green" colors. Incidentally, here the mark includes a claim to color and the colors must be included in the design drawing.

Letters like numbers are strong trademarks when they have no recognizable descriptive meaning. The absence of recognizable meaning amongst a combination of letters, such as television and radio call letters for instance, makes a mere rudimentary change in a letter over a letter combination that has trademark protection may not be enough to avoid confusion. However, when letter combinations are shown to convey a different meaning, likelihood of confusion cannot be found.

Other Types of Marks

Trade Names

In addition to trademarks and service marks, the Lanham Act also defines other types of marks. A "trade name" also known as a "commercial name" is any name in use to identify a business or vocation. Often, organizations merely drop the corporation's legal identification indicia such as "Company" or "LLC," and merely use the given name as the trade name. For example, Apple Inc. or Apple Music, or Apple TV+ for example are collectively simply referred to as "Apple" in essence establishing a doing business as ("d/b/a") name. However, merely registering a d/b/a name as a trade name does not provide the same level of protection as a trademark, but a trade name may eventually be recognized as a trademark as a source identifier of the company's products or services.

Certification Mark

A "certification mark" is used to certify certain product characteristics such as, for example, regional origin; standards relating to quality, material or mode of manufacture; and labor being performed by a certain union. Certification marks are not owned by the certifying authority and they do not identify the commercial source of such products even though there are certain requirements that must be met before a party can adopt the use of the certification mark for use in association with a product. For example, COGNAC identifies a distilled brandy from a region of France, and TEQUILLA may only be used in association with alcoholic beverages made in accordance with Mexican law, but not necessarily manufactured in Mexico.

Collective Mark

A "collective mark" is a trademark or service mark used by members of a cooperative, association, or other collective group or organization having a bona fide intention to use the collective mark in commerce. Collective marks may indicate membership in a union, an association or other organization.

Collective marks may be used by particular members of the organization that owns them, while certification marks are the only evidence of the existence of follow-up agreements between manufacturers and nationally accredited testing and certification organizations. Many times, owners of certification marks have written standards that must be complied with before a product or service can become associated with the use of the certification mark. Examples of such organizations having certification marks include the American National Standards Institute or ANSI® and Underwriter's Laboratories or UL. Underwriter's Laboratories, for example, has been somewhat diligent in protecting the use of it mark in association with certifications.

On some occasions, the certification organization will charge for the use of their labels and will require that the manufacturer reports the exact production quantities. Certain certification organizations require the purchase of their standards reporting the tests that must be conducted to comply with the use of the certification mark.

Trade Dress

The Lanham Act represents that trade dress encompasses almost anything at all that is capable of carrying meaning, but the trade dress may not be functional. While trade dress may be trademarked, in some cases, most usually, trade dress enjoys protection without registration. In fact, whenever trademark infringement claims are asserted in a lawsuit, it is also quite common for the plaintiff to assert trade dress claims as well even if the trade dress is not registered.

The Supreme Court has been involved in helping to more clearly define what trade dress encompasses. In *Two Pesos v. Taco Cabana*, a 1992 case, the Supreme Court found that Taco Cabana's Mexican restaurant chain's decor is inherently distinctive because, in addition to murals and bright colored pottery typically found in Mexican restaurants, the chain also uses a specific indoor and outdoor decor based upon primarily pink neon colored border stripes, distinctive outdoor umbrellas, and a novel buffet style of service.[5] Two Pesos was found to have infringed upon Taco Cabana's trade dress.

Taco Cabana

Two Pesos

[5] *Two Pesos, Inc. v. Taco Cabana, Inc.*, 505 U.S. 763 (1992).

On the other hand, the Supreme Court has found that product designs such as the appearance of a line of children's clothing are not inherently distinctive and can only be protected if they eventually acquire distinctiveness through sales or advertising.[6]

The seminal case concerning functionality of trade dress involved temporary road signs capable of withstanding strong gusts of wind.[7] The Supreme Court determined that the dual-spring design of the road signs serves the important purpose of keeping the sign upright even in heavy wind conditions, and the feature is functional, notwithstanding its notable design, because the design including the dual-springs is essential to the use or purpose of the device. It was also determined that the effective dual-spring design affected the cost or quality of the device. Therefore, the Supreme Court found that the trade dress encompassed within the road sign is functional in nature and cannot be protected as trade dress.

Preceding the Supreme Court's decision in *Traffix*, the Second Circuit Court of Appeals found that functionality of the Brandir Ribbon Rack, a bicycle rack made of bent tubing, a design feature performs a function itself does not make it essential to the performance of that function, but rather it is instead the absence of alternative constructions performing the same function that renders the feature functional.[8] Thus, the true test of functionality is not whether the feature in question performs a function, but whether the feature is

---

[6] *Wal-Mart Stores, Inc. v. Samara Brothers, Inc.*, 529 U.S. 205 (2000).
[7] *Traffix Devices Inc. v. Marketing Displays Inc.*, 532 U.S. 23, 121 S.Ct. 1255, 149 L.Ed.2d 164 (2001).
[8] *Brandir Intern., Inc. v. Cascade Pacific Lumber Co.*, 834 F.2d 1142 (2nd Cir., 1987).

dictated by the functions to be performed. The Second Circuit Court of Appeals remanded the case to the district court for a determination of functionality based upon the precedent they established with respect to the Ribbon Rack.

CHAPTER 3: International Classification of Goods and Services

Nice Classification

Trademarks are registered based upon one or more classes depending upon the desired extent of use of the mark. The *International Classification of Goods and Services for the Purposes of the Registration of Marks* (current version: 10th ed. 2011) is set via the Nice Agreement and the classifications are published by the World Intellectual Property Organization ("WIPO"). As will be further discussed in Chapter 7, it would be difficult to find that a mark infringes a registered trademark if the goods or services associated with that mark fails to fit within the class where the trademark is registered. The primary exception to this rubric is with respect to the concept of dilution. Dilution applies to marks that have become famous and another commences use of a mark that would likely cause dilution through blurring or tarnishment regardless of the presence or absence of a likelihood of confusion.

Famous marks are those marks that are widely recognized by the general consuming public of the United States as a designation of source of the goods or services of the mark's owner. The following factors may serve as a guide in the court's determination of whether a mark has become famous or not: (i) duration, extent, and geographic reach of advertising and publicity of the mark, whether advertised or publicized by the owner or third parties, (ii) amount, volume, and geographic extent of sales of goods or services offered under the mark, (iii) extent of actual recognition of the mark, and (iv) whether the mark was registered under the earlier acts of March 3, 1881, or February 20, 1905 or under the principal register of the Lanham Act (latter register is discussed in more detail in Chapter 5). In actual precedent, a showing that a mark is famous has proven difficult.

The purpose of the international list is to classify goods and services and not to identify specific goods and services. The registrant is responsible for proposing a description of their goods and services that fit within a proposed class and it becomes the task of the Examiner at the USPTO to determine whether the description properly fits within the class or not.

Currently, there are 45 classes within the International Classification System with classes 1 to 34 related to goods and classes 35 to 45 related to services. The current list is accessible via the USPTO.[1]

The definitions of classes in the International Classification System is quite comprehensive and include many subclasses. The purpose of this chapter is to provide an overview of each of the classes and to give some examples of trademarks and the associated products or services that fit within that class. The general heading identifications used for each of the classes have been taken from the Trademark Manual of Examining Procedure (TMEP), the guide used by the USPTO to provide trademark examining attorneys in the USPTO, trademark applicants, and attorneys and representatives for trademark applicants with a reference work on the practices and procedures relative to prosecution of applications to register marks in the USPTO. The Manual contains guidelines for Examining Attorneys and materials in the nature of information and interpretation, and outlines the procedures which Examining Attorneys are required or authorized to follow in the examination of trademark applications. The current version of the TMEP is available for online for review and download.[2]

---

1 http://www.uspto.gov/trademark/trademark-updates-and-announcements/ nice-agreement-tenth-edition-general-remarks-class

2 http://tmep.uspto.gov/RDMS/TMEP/current#/current/d1e2.html

Int'l Class 01 – Chemicals

Chemicals used in industry, science and photography, as well as in agriculture, horticulture and forestry; unprocessed artificial resins, unprocessed plastics; manures; fire extinguishing compositions; tempering and soldering preparations; chemical substances for preserving foodstuffs; tanning substances; adhesives used in industry.

Class 01 has 684 subclasses similar to the following examples:

010106 bases [chemical preparations]
010126 basic gallate of bismuth
010208 bate for dressing skins / dressing, except oils, for skins
010108 bauxite
010619 beer preserving agent

VISTAMAXX® to Exxon Mobile Corporation used in association with polymers used in the manufacture of adhesives, nonwoven fabrics, films, packaging, food and beverage containers, construction products, medical equipment, automotive and consumer products; and Pi K Si Dust to PiKSi Dust Co, LLC used in association with fertilizers containing potassium and silicon are examples of marks registered in Int'l Class 01.

Int'l Class 02 – Paints

Paints, varnishes, lacquers; preservatives against rust and against deterioration of wood; colorants, dyes; inks for printing, marking and engraving; raw natural resins; metals in foil and powder form for use in painting, decorating, printing and art.

Class 02 has 116 subclasses similar to the following examples:

020001 paints
020096 paper for dyeing Easter eggs
020059 pigments
020108 primers
020043 printers' pastes [ink]
020066 printing ink

GLIDDEN® to Akzo Nobel Paints LLC used in association with coating compositions, namely, paints, varnishes and lacquers; and the WD-40 can shown here to the WD-40 Manufacturing Company used in association with protective coatings for rust prevention and corrosion control are examples of marks registered in Int'l Class 02.

Int'l Class 03 – Cosmetics and Cleaning Preparations

Non-medicated cosmetics and toiletry preparations; non-medicated dentifrices; perfumery, esscntial oils; bleaching preparations and other substances for laundry use; cleaning, polishing, scouring and abrasive preparations.

Class 03 has 237 subclasses similar to the following examples:

030135 perfumes
030047 polish for furniture and flooring
030203 potpourris [fragrances]
030170 rust removing preparations
030140 sandpaper / glass paper
030091 scented water
030076 scouring solutions
030134 shampoos

PANTENE® to The Procter & Gamble Company used in association with hair conditioning, styling mousse, hair styling gel and hair spray; and Old Spice to Shulton, Inc. used in association with antiperspirants and deodorants for personal use, body sprays, fragrances, hair care preparations, bath soaps in liquid, solid or gel form are examples of marks registered in Int'l Class 03.

Int'l Class 04 – Lubricants and Fuels

Industrial oils and greases, wax; lubricants; dust absorbing, wetting and binding compositions; fuels and illuminants; candles and wicks for lighting.

Class 04 has 237 subclasses similar to the following examples:

040087 industrial oil
040059 kerosene
040041 lighting fuel
040063 lubricants
040032 mineral fuel
040104 motor oil
040076 nightlights [candles]
040050 oil-gas
040102 oils for paints
040070 paraffin

VALVOLINE® to Ashland Oil Refining Company used in association with petroleum products for use in connection with vehicles operated by motive power and in connection with engines and machinery, and to National Biofuels Distribution LLC used in association with fuel are examples of marks registered in Int'l Class 04.

Int'l Class 05 – Pharmaceuticals

Pharmaceuticals, medical and veterinary preparations; sanitary preparations for medical purposes; dietetic food and substances adapted for medical or veterinary use, food for babies; dietary supplements for human beings and animals; plasters, materials for dressings; material for stopping teeth, dental wax; disinfectants; preparations for destroying vermin; fungicides, herbicides.

Class 05 has 458 subclasses similar to the following examples:

050069 pharmaceutical preparations
050100 pharmaceutical preparations for treating sunburn
050239 pharmaceutical preparations for skin care
050241 pharmaceutical preparations for treating dandruff
050453 pharmaceuticals
050249 poisons
050115 porcelain for dental prostheses
050449 powdered milk for babies
050462 pre-filled syringes for medical purposes

050435 protein dietary supplements
050258 radioactive substances for medical purposes
050464 reagent paper for veterinary purposes
050411 preparations for reducing sexual activity
050247 remedies for foot perspiration
050042 salts for mineral water baths
050232 sanitary tampons / menstruation tampons

ALKA-SELTZER® to Bayer Healthcare, LLC used in association with dietary supplement for aiding sleep and antacids, and  to Sanofi used in association with pharmaceutical preparations for the treatment and prevention of central nervous system diseases and conditions are examples of marks registered in Int'l Class 05.

Int'l Class 06 – Metal Goods

Common metals and their alloys, ores; metal materials for building and construction; transportable buildings of metal; non-electric cables and wires of common metal; small items of metal hardware; metal containers for storage or transport; safes.

Class 06 has 444 subclasses similar to the following examples:

060434 metals in powder form
060474 mouldings / moldings of metal for building
060085 nails
060399 nameplates of metal / identity plates of metal
060364 nuts of metal
060231 packaging containers of metal
060062 padlocks
060141 pins [hardware]
060127 pipes of metal / tubes of metal
060226 platforms, prefabricated, of metal
060024 poles of metal

REYNOLDS WRAP® to Reynolds Metal Company used in association with aluminum foil sheets and rolls, and PICTURE HANG to Art

Hardware, LLC used in association with metal hardware, namely, D-rings, hangers, screws and cleats for use in attaching and hanging items to walls are examples of marks registered in Int'l Class 06.

Int'l Class 07 – Machinery

Machines, machine tools, power-operated tools; motors and engines, except for land vehicles; machine coupling and transmission components, except for land vehicles; agricultural implements, other than hand-operated hand tools; incubators for eggs; automatic vending machines.

Class 07 has 556 subclasses similar to the following examples:

070415 coffee grinders, other than hand-operated
070236 coin-operated washing machines
070113 compressors [machines]
070045 concrete mixers [machines]
070435 control mechanisms for machines, engines or motors
070472 hydraulic controls for machines, motors and engines
070371 conveyors [machines]
070453 cranes [lifting and hoisting apparatus]
070230 cranks [parts of machines]
070146 cutting machines
070139 cylinders for machines
070397 diggers [machines]
070231 dishwashers
070539 door openers, electric
070012 apparatus for drawing up beer under pressure

MOW N'STOW® to Briggs & Stratton Corporation used in association with engines for lawnmowers and walk behind lawn mowers; and  to Ningbo Chefshere Kitchen Technology Co, Ltd used in association with, *inter alia*, coffee grinders are examples of marks registered in Int'l Class 07.

Int'l Class 08 – Hand Tools

Hand tools and implements, hand-operated; cutlery; side arms, except firearms; razors.

Class 08 has 264 subclasses similar to the following examples:

080156 hammers [hand tools]
080072 hand tools, hand-operated
080137 hatchets
080185 hoes [hand tools]
080053 hunting knives
080127 lawn clippers [hand instruments]
080231 manicure sets
080249 pizza cutters, non-electric
080206 pliers
080109 rakes [hand tools]
080148 razor blades
080179 razors, electric or non-electric
080055 saws [hand tools]
080040 scissors
080195 screwdrivers, non-electric
080110 shovels [hand tools]
080022 side arms, other than firearms
080157 sledgehammers

TREE BRAND® to Heinrich Boker Baumwerk GmbH used in association with pocket knives, fixed blade knives, folding knives, straight razors, multi-function hand tools comprised of knives, throwing knives, hunting knives; and to The Gillette Company LLC used in association with razor blade cartridges are examples of marks registered in Int'l Class 08.

Int'l Class 09 – Electrical and Scientific Apparatus

Scientific, research, navigation, surveying, photographic, cinematographic, audiovisual, optical, weighing, measuring, signaling, detecting, testing, inspecting, life-saving and teaching apparatus and instruments; apparatus and instruments for conducting, switching, transforming, accumulating, regulating or controlling the distribution or use of electricity; apparatus and instruments for recording, transmitting, reproducing or processing sound, images or data; recorded and downloadable media, computer software, blank digital or analogue recording and storage media; mechanisms for coin-operated apparatus; cash registers, calculating devices; computers and computer peripheral devices; diving suits, divers' masks, ear plugs for divers, nose clips for divers and swimmers, gloves for divers, breathing apparatus for underwater swimming; fire-extinguishing apparatus.

Class 09 has 752 subclasses similar to the following examples:

090347 measuring instruments
090727 memory cards for video game machines
090348 meteorological instruments
090351 microphones
090610 microprocessors
090193 microscopes
090734 mobile telephones / cell phones / cellular phones
090612 monitors [computer hardware]
090358 navigational instruments
090330 neon signs
090642 notebook computers
090154 photocopiers [photographic, electrostatic, thermic]
090394 photo telegraphy apparatus
090644 pocket calculators
090346 precision measuring apparatus
090410 pressure indicators
090699 printed circuit boards
090618 printers for use with computers

THE CLEAR REVOLUTION® to Sportsgear Outdoor Products LLC used in association with binoculars, laser range finders, spotting scopes, telescopes, telescopic bow sights for archery, archery equipment, namely, telescopic bow sights, hunting binoculars, prisms, reflecting telescopes, tripods; and to

Captora LLC used in association with computer software for use in customer relationship management (CRM) are examples of marks registered in Int'l Class 09.

Int'l Class 10 – Medical Apparatus
Surgical, medical, dental and veterinary apparatus and instruments; artificial limbs, eyes and teeth; orthopedic articles; suture materials; therapeutic and assistive devices adapted for the disabled; massage apparatus; apparatus, devices and articles for nursing infants; sexual activity apparatus, devices and articles.

Class 10 has 260 subclasses similar to the following examples:

100020 bandages for joints, anatomical / supportive bandages
100022 bandages, elastic
100025 bed pans
100173 beds specially made for medical purposes
100087 blood testing apparatus
100252 bracelets for medical purposes
100200 clothing especially for operating rooms
100168 crutches
100211 defibrillators
100073 dental apparatus and instruments
100084 electrocardiographs
100028 feeding bottles / babies' bottles
100043 gloves for medical purposes
100203 heart pacemakers
100029 knives for surgical purposes
100258 magnetic resonance imaging [MRI] apparatus for medical purposes
100205 masks for use by medical personnel

FLOWSMART® to Becton, Dickinson and Company used in association with a feature of subcutaneous infusion sets for use by diabetes patients in connection with insulin pumps, and to Terumo Kabushiki Kaisha a/k/a Terumo Corporation used in association with medical syringes, prefillable medical syringes, sold empty are examples of marks registered in Int'l Class 10.

<u>Int'l Class 11 – Environmental Control Apparatus</u>
Apparatus and installations for lighting, heating, cooling, steam generating, cooking, drying, ventilating, water supply and sanitary purposes.

Class 11 has 333 subclasses similar to the following examples:

110079 air conditioners for vehicles
110207 air purifying apparatus and machines
110014 air-conditioning installations
110307 aquarium filtration apparatus
110265 barbecues
110033 bath tubs
110136 ceiling lights
110262 coffee machines, electric
110354 electric cooktops
110266 deep fryers, electric
110065 fans [air-conditioning]
110147 filters for drinking water
110267 fireplaces, domestic
110106 freezers
110150 furnaces, other than for laboratory use / ovens, other than for laboratory use
110095 hair dryers / hair driers
110167 ice machines and apparatus
110040 lamps
110021 light bulbs
110256 lights for automobiles / automobile lights

THE HEALTHY KITCHEN® to Lenox Corporation d/b/a Dansk used in association with air purifiers, electric food steamer, electric rice cooker, electric slow cookers; and  to Delta T, LLC used in association with ventilating fans for commercial and industrial use are examples of marks registered in Int'l Class 11.

Int'l Class 12 – Vehicles

Vehicles; apparatus for locomotion by land, air or water.

Class 12 has 294 subclasses similar to the following examples:

120184 aircraft
120271 armoured / armored vehicles
120044 bicycles
120021 boats
120199 cars / motor cars / automobiles
120068 golf carts [vchicles] / golf cars [vehicles]
120144 military vehicles for transport

MUSTANG® to Ford Motor Company used in association with automobiles and their structural parts, and to Cummins, Inc. used in association with engines for land vehicles, motors for land vehicles are examples of marks registered in Int'l Class 12.

Int'l Class 13 – Firearms

Firearms; ammunition and projectiles; explosives; fireworks.

Class 13 has 75 subclasses similar to the following examples:

130027 ammunition
130020 cannons
130032 dynamite
130034 explosives
130009 firearms
130013 fireworks
130036 guns [weapons]
130026 hunting firearms / sporting firearms
130049 pistols [arms]

WRANGLER® to Sturm, Ruger & Company, Inc. used in association with firearms and revolvers, and to American Promotional Events, Inc. d/b/a TNT Fireworks used in association with fireworks are examples of marks registered in Int'l Class 13.

Int'l Class 14 – Jewelry

Precious metals and their alloys; jewelry, precious and semi-precious stones; horological and chronometric instruments.

Class 14 has 100 subclasses similar to the following examples:

140024 chains [jewellery] / chains [jewelry]
140011 clocks
140034 coins
140035 diamonds
140118 earrings
140003 ingots of precious metals
140050 jewellery / jewelry
140166 jewellery boxes / jewelry boxes
140031 necklaces [jewellery] / necklaces [jewelry]
140070 pearls [jewellery] / pearls [jewelry]
140055 precious metals, unwrought or semi-wrought
140074 precious stones

OYSTERSTEEL® to Rolex Watch U.S.A., Inc. used in association with watches and parts thereof, comprised in whole or significant part of steel; and to Oro Brand Inc. used in association with jewelry, rings, bracelets, necklaces, pendants, earrings are examples of marks registered in Int'l Class 14.

Int'l Class 15 – Musical Instruments

Musical instruments; music stands and stands for musical instruments; conductors' batons.

Class 15 has 94 subclasses similar to the following examples:

150051 bagpipes
150091 banjos
150066 drums [musical instruments]
150036 flutes
150039 guitars

150041 harps
150030 horns [musical instruments]
150024 keyboards for musical instruments
150057 organs
150008 pianos
150089 saxophones

ELITE® to Ovation Instruments, Inc. used in association with guitars, and to BP Trumpets LLC used in association with musical instrument accessories, namely, stands, cases, carrying bags and storage bags, musical instruments, namely, trumpets, cornets, and flugelhorns, replacement parts and fittings for musical instruments are examples of marks registered in Int'l Class 15.

Int'l Class 16 – Paper Goods and Printed Matter

Paper and cardboard; printed matter; bookbinding material; photographs; stationery and office requisites, except furniture; adhesives for stationery or household purposes; drawing materials and materials for artists; paintbrushes; instructional and teaching materials; plastic sheets, films and bags for wrapping and packaging; printers' type, printing blocks.

Class 16 has 357 subclasses similar to the following examples:

160323 bags for microwave cooking
160223 blueprints / plans
160189 booklets
160095 books
160075 cardboard
160124 drawing materials
160127 envelopes [stationery]
160225 fountain pens
160250 greeting cards
160243 magazines [periodicals]
160032 newspapers
160030 paintings [pictures], framed or unframed
160006 paper

COPY PLUS® to Hammern pany used in association with copy paper, and to Cointegrity, Inc. used in association with paper punches for office use, namely, coin roll wrapper crimp modifiers are examples of marks registered in Int'l Class 16.

Int'l Class 17 – Rubber Goods

Unprocessed and semi-processed rubber, gutta-percha, gum, asbestos, mica and substitutes for all these materials; plastics and resins in extruded form for use in manufacture; packing, stopping and insulating materials; flexible pipes, tubes and hoses, not of metal.

Class 17 has 120 subclasses similar to the following examples:

170077 bags [envelopes, pouches] of rubber, for packaging
170040 caulking materials
170042 chemical compositions for repairing leaks
170118 duct tapes
170023 insulating materials
170072 plastic film, other than for wrapping
170089 reinforcing materials, not of metal, for pipes
170114 rubber solutions

E/FUSOMG® to Midsun Specialty Products, Inc. used in association with silicon rubber electrical tape; and to Odenwald-Chemie GmbH used in association with plastics in pressed and extruded form for use in manufacture, packing, thermal insulating and acoustic insulating materials made of plastics, raw and semi-worked rubber, natural rubber, EPDM, gutta percha, fleece and polyurethane foam, polypropylene and polyethylene foam, sealing materials made of plastics, raw and semi-worked rubber, natural rubber, gutta percha, fleece and polyurethane foam and polyethylene foam, flexible pipes, not of metal are examples of marks registered in Int'l Class 17.

Int'l Class 18 – Leather Goods

Leather and imitations of leather; animal skins and hides; luggage and carrying bags; umbrellas and parasols; walking sticks; whips, harness and saddlery; collars, leashes and clothing for animals.

Class 18 has 123 subclasses similar to the following examples:

180124 bags
180112 bridles [harness]
180083 briefcases
180126 business card cases
180125 credit card cases [wallets]
180111 garment bags for travel
180077 handbags
180005 leather leashes / leather leads

BROOME STREET® to Kate Spade, LLC used in association with all-purpose carrying bags, animal carriers, animal leashes, athletic bags, sports bags, backpacks, beach bags, book bags, briefcases, clutches, coin purses, cosmetic bags sold empty, cosmetic cases sold empty, diaper bags, document cases, duffel bags, evening handbags, fanny packs, handbags, key cases, luggage and trunks, luggage tags, plastic luggage labels, messenger bags, wheeled messenger bags, pet clothing, pet collar accessories, namely, charms, purses, shoulder bags, tote bags, travel bags, umbrellas, wallets, wristlet bags, business card holders in the nature of wallets and card cases, fitted protective covers for handbags, briefcases, suitcases, and briefcase-like portfolios; and to Luci Bags LLC used in association with tote bags are examples of marks registered in Int'l Class 18.

Int'l Class 19 – Non-metallic Building Materials

Materials, not of metal, for building and construction; rigid pipes, not of metal, for building; asphalt, pitch, tar and bitumen; transportable buildings, not of metal; monuments, not of metal.

Class 19 has 257 subclasses similar to the following examples:

190036 cement
190055 chimneys, not of metal
190051 materials for making and coating roads
190023 concrete
190069 doors, not of metal
190147 floors, not of metal
190167 greenhouses, transportable, not of metal
190120 marble
190089 memorial plaques, not of metal
190117 monuments, not of metal

ADVANTAGE PLUS® to Pella Corporation used in association with exterior weather protection features for nonmetal doors, namely, a frame with a protective finish and aluminum exterior trim, designed with the door and frames placed on top of the sill, all as an integral part of nonmetal doors; and to Giant Cement Holding, Inc. used in association with masonry cement are examples of marks registered in Int'l Class 19.

Int'l Class 20 – Furniture and Articles not Otherwise Classified
Furniture, mirrors, picture frames; containers, not of metal, for storage or transport; unworked or semi-worked bone, horn, whalebone or mother-of-pearl; shells; meerschaum; yellow amber.

Class 20 has 314 subclasses similar to the following examples:
200102 beds
200020 benches [furniture]
200309 bookcases
200088 cabinet work
200066 chests of drawers
200036 desks
200041 furniture
200079 mattresses
200037 office furniture

SEKTION® to Inter-IKEA Systems B.V. used in association with kitchen cabinets, and parts and fittings therefor, namely, doors, legs, and drawers; and the mattress image 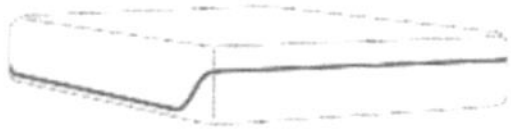 to Tempur World, LLC used in association with mattresses featuring a memory-foam mattress with a removable cover, sold as a unit are examples of marks registered in Int'l Class 20.

Int'l Class 21 – Housewares and Glass

Household or kitchen utensils and containers; cookware and tableware, except forks, knives and spoons; combs and sponges; brushes, except paintbrushes; brush-making materials; articles for cleaning purposes; unworked or semi-worked glass, except building glass; glassware, porcelain and earthenware.

Class 21 has 376 subclasses similar to the following examples:

210259 abrasive pads for kitchen purposes
210233 aerosol dispensers, not for medical purposes
210096 blenders, non-electric, for household purposes
210048 bottle openers, electric and non-electric
210045 bottles
210020 brooms
210014 brushes
210021 carpet sweepers
210104 cleaning instruments, hand-operated
210254 coffee grinders, hand-operated
210076 combs
210317 cookie jars
210318 cups of paper or plastic

LIQUID-PLUMR® to The Clorox Company used in association with plungers for clearing blocked drains; and [Scotch-Brite logo] to 3M Company used in association with scouring, cleaning and scrubbing sponges, pads and brushes, scouring, cleaning and scrubbing sponges, pads and brushes, all featuring handles, cleaning cloths [and disposable textile cleaning wipes] not impregnated with chemicals or compounds, dusting cloths [and mitts], mops and brooms are examples of marks registered in Int'l Class 21.

<u>Int'l Class 22 – Cordage and Fibers</u>
Ropes and string; nets; tents and tarpaulins; awnings of textile or synthetic materials; sails; sacks for the transport and storage of materials in bulk; padding, cushioning and stuffing materials, except of paper, cardboard, rubber or plastics; raw fibrous textile materials and substitutes therefor.

Class 22 has 106 subclasses similar to the following examples:

220084 cables, not of metal
220087 carbon fibres / fibers for textile use
220089 cords for hanging pictures
220025 raw cotton
220028 down [feathers]
220011 fishing nets
220072 fleece wool
220043 hammocks
220013 hemp
220104 mail bags
220106 mesh bags for washing laundry

POLY-FIL® to Fairfield Processing Corporation used in association with polyester batting, filling material suitable for filling pillows, toys, upholstery, comforters, and the like, namely, expanded polystyrene beads, cushioning of synthetic fiber batting in the nature of stuffing for chair cushions, deck furniture, camping and boat cushions, futons, upholstery, crib bumpers and the like, processed synthetic polypropylene stuffing material used for stuffing dolls, toys, pillows, upholstery, comforters and the like, processed synthetic fiber, polyester fibers used in filling dolls, toys, pillows, upholstery, comforters, and the like; and KNOT STRAP SOLUTIONS to Artefita - Indústria de Passamanarias used in association with all-purpose straps comprised of synthetic textile materials, nylon strapping or tiedowns, and nylon straps for handling loads are examples of marks registered in Int'l Class 22.

Int'l Class 23 – Yarns and Threads

Yarns and threads for textile use.

Class 23 has 44 subclasses similar to the following examples:

230002 cotton thread and yarn
230017 fibreglass /fiberglass thread for textile use
230005 hemp thread and yarn
230009 sewing thread and yarn
230007 silk thread and yarn
230008 spun cotton
230012 spun wool / worsted
230016 spun silk

BOLTSPUN® to Bolt Threads, Inc. used in association with materials for making textiles, apparel and home furnishings, natural protein fiber yarn and thread, natural protein yarns, fiber yarn and thread made of proteins, customizable yarns, threads, and fiber yarn and thread made of proteins, spider silk thread, and to Bambary Corp used in association with sewing thread are examples of marks registered in Int'l Class 23.

Int'l Class 24 – Fabrics

Textiles and substitutes for textiles; household linen; curtains of textile or plastic.

Class 24 has 118 subclasses similar to the following examples:

240006 banners of textile or plastic
240005 bath linen, except clothing
240029 bed covers / bedspreads / coverlets [bedspreads] / quilts
240068 bed linen
240114 bed blankets
240111 chenille fabric
240013 cloth

240028 cotton fabrics
240085 curtains of textile or plastic
240046 elastic woven material
240008 fabric
240117 furniture coverings of textile
240019 hat linings, of textile, in the piece
240067 linen cloth
240098 non-woven textile fabrics
240040 sheets [textile]
240088 silk [cloth]
240012 textile material
240064 woolen cloth / woolen fabric

SUNNY FABRIC® to Gauze Fabric Store used in association with gauze fabric, and to LuLu DK Lifestyle, LLC used in association with bedding in the nature of bed blankets, bed sheets and comforters, towels, pillows, pillow cases, pillow covers, shams, and fabrics for textile use are examples of marks registered in Int'l Class 24.

<u>Int'l Class 25 – Clothing</u>
Clothing, footwear, headwear.

Class 25 has 175 subclasses similar to the following examples:

250148 bandanas [neckerchiefs]
250127 bath robes
250126 bathing suits / swimsuits
250014 boots
250045 clothing
250086 coats
250109 dresses
250003 footwear
250067 gloves [clothing]
250046 hats
250013 hosiery
250060 neckties

250111 sandals
250042 shirts
250130 shoes
250036 socks
250056 suits
250034 sweaters / pullovers / jumpers [pullovers]
250155 tee-shirts
250026 underwear / underclothing

TIGHT STUFF® to Lululemon Athletica Canada Inc. used in association with clothing, namely, pants, tights, and leggings; and

to Garden State Baseball, L.P. used in association with clothing, namely, aprons, athletic uniforms, bandanas, caps being headwear, coats, golf shirts, gym shorts, hats, jackets, jerseys, polo shirts, pullovers, sweat shirts, socks, sport shirts, t-shirts, tank tops, ties, and visors being headwear are examples of marks registered in Int'l Class 25.

<u>Int'l Class 26 – Fancy Goods</u>

Lace, braid and embroidery, and haberdashery ribbons and bows; buttons, hooks and eyes, pins and needles; artificial flowers; hair decorations; false hair.

Class 26 has 128 subclasses similar to the following examples:

260059 artificial flowers
260114 bows for the hair
260021 buttons
260028 embroidery / fancy goods [embroidery]
260013 hair bands
260125 hair extensions
260034 shoelaces
260093 silver embroidery
260089 toupees
260079 wigs

CUFFUP® to Qingdao Wanguojinji e-commerce Co., Ltd used in association with arm bands; artificial flowers of plastics, artificial flowers of textile, artificial plants, other than Christmas trees, artificial wreaths; buttons for clothing, clothing accessories, namely, charms for attachment to zipper pulls and buttons, clothing buckles, elastic ribbons, frills for attachment to clothing, trimmings for clothing; and the "BOBBI BOSS" design to Midway International, Inc. used in association with hair extensions, hairpieces, and wigs constructed primarily of synthetic and/or human hair are examples of marks registered in Int'l Class 26.

Int'l Class 27 – Floor Coverings

Carpets, rugs, mats and matting, linoleum and other materials for covering existing floors; wall hangings, not of textile.

Class 27 has 21 subclasses similar to the following examples:

270015 carpet underlay
270011 carpets / rugs
270013 decorative wall hangings, not of textile
270002 floor coverings
270006 mats
270007 wallpaper

ADAPTEX® to Milliken & Company used in association with floor coverings, floormats, floor coverings with a predominantly textile top that detaches from the bottom of the floor covering, sold as a unit or sold as separate top and bottom components; and to Spencer 1508 Limited used in association with carpets, rugs, mats and matting, linoleum for covering existing floors, non-textile wall hangings, wallpaper, bath mats are examples of marks registered in Int'l Class 27.

Int'l Class 28 – Toys and Sporting Goods

Games, toys and playthings; video game apparatus; gymnastic and sporting articles; decorations for Christmas trees.

Class 28 has 241 subclasses similar to the following examples:

280189 amusement machines, automatic and coin-operated
280123 billiard tables
280156 board games
280006 Christmas trees of synthetic material
280217 controllers for game consoles
280088 dolls
280083 fishing tackle
280084 fishing lines
280079 games
280034 golf clubs
280256 hand-held consoles for playing video games
280045 novelty toys for parties
280119 ornaments for Christmas trees, except illumination articles and confectionery
280043 machines for physical exercises
280035 rods for fishing
280198 scale model kits [toys]
280148 skateboards
280010 swings
280151 teddy bears
280163 toy vehicles
280024 toys
280255 video game consoles

BARBIE® to Mattel, Inc. used in association with full line of dolls, doll clothing and doll accessories; and to Ninka Holdings, LLC used in association with sporting articles, namely, esports-related sporting articles in the nature of gaming gloves, toy action figures and toy action figure accessories, console game controllers, namely, hand-held game consoles and controllers for game consoles, playing cards, board games, role playing games, water toys, plush toys, radio-controlled toy vehicles and drone toys, party games, headphones and computer peripherals used in connection with video games and videogame systems, gaming headgear adapted for use in playing videogames, namely, esports headgear, trading cards for games are examples of marks registered in Int'l Class 28.

<u>Int'l Class 29 – Meats and Processed Foods</u>
Meat, fish, poultry and game; meat extracts; preserved, frozen, dried and cooked fruits and vegetables; jellies, jams, compotes; eggs; milk, cheese, butter, yoghurt and other milk products; oils and fats for food.

Class 29 has 220 subclasses similar to the following examples:

290076 bacon
290014 broth / bouillon
290008 butter
290034 cheese
290086 eggs
290047 fish, not live
290003 gelatine
290078 margarine
290046 meat

NAKED MEATS® to Swift Brands Company used in association with all natural, preservative-free, antibiotic-free, luncheon meats from humanely-raised animals; and LOUIS KEMP SEAFOOD Co. to Oscar Meyer Foods Corporation used in association with surimi seafood, processed fish or imitation seafood are examples of marks registered in Int'l Class 29.

<u>Int'l Class 30 – Staple Foods</u>
Coffee, tea, cocoa and artificial coffee; rice, pasta and noodles; tapioca and sago; flour and preparations made from cereals; bread, pastries and confectionery; chocolate; ice cream, sorbets and other edible ices; sugar, honey, treacle; yeast, baking-powder; salt, seasonings, spices, preserved herbs; vinegar, sauces and other condiments; ice (frozen water).

Class 30 has 255 subclasses similar to the following examples:

300093 bread
300072 cake batter / cake dough
300203 cake frosting [icing]
300035 chewing gum
300026 coffee
300174 crackers
300188 dressings for salad
300057 flour / meal
300098 honey
300186 iced tea
300082 ketchup [sauce]
300133 meat pies
300103 noodles / ribbon vermicelli
300047 pancakes
300217 pasta sauce
300104 pies
300112 pizzas

FOLGERS® to The Folger Coffee Company used in association with coffee, and to Imo's Franchising, Inc. used in association with chicken wing sauce, salad dressing, pizza sauce, pizza shells and frozen pizza are examples of marks registered in Int'l Class 30.

<u>Int'l Class 31 – Natural Agriculture Products</u>

Raw and unprocessed agricultural, aquacultural, horticultural and forestry products; raw and unprocessed grains and seeds; fresh fruits and vegetables, fresh herbs; natural plants and flowers; bulbs, seedlings and seeds for planting; live animals; foodstuffs and beverages for animals; malt.

Class 31 has 161 subclasses similar to the following examples:

310148 aloe vera plants
310007 animal foodstuffs
310013 berries, fresh

310035 bird food
310009 Christmas trees
310002 citrus fruit, fresh
310103 fish, live
310055 flowers, natural
310062 fruit, fresh
310080 litter for animals
310088 meal for animals

LONESTAR NUT® to L'Orenta Holding, LLC used in association with nuts, namely, raw nuts, fresh nuts, unprocessed nuts, and  to Full Waters LLC used in association with beverages for animals are examples of marks registered in Int'l Class 31.

<u>Int'l Class 32 – Light Beverages</u>
Beers; non-alcoholic beverages; mineral and aerated waters; fruit beverages and fruit juices; syrups and other non-alcoholic preparations for making beverages.

Class 32 has 51 subclasses similar to the following examples:
320002 beer
320035 carbonated water / aerated water
320047 cider, non-alcoholic
320010 fruit juices / fruit juice
320020 lemonades
320031 non-alcoholic beverages
320017 seltzer water
320058 soft drinks
320022 vegetable juices [beverages]
320012 waters [beverages]

DEER PARK® to Nestle Waters North America Inc. used in association with drinking water, and 

to Old River Brewing

Company used in association with beer are examples of marks registered in Int'l Class 32.

Int'l Class 33 – Wines and Spirits
Alcoholic beverages, except beers; alcoholic preparations for making beverages.

Class 33 has 33 subclasses similar to the following examples:

330026 alcoholic beverages, except beer
330031 alcoholic beverages containing fruit
330019 brandy
330009 cider
330008 distilled beverages
330015 liqueurs
330018 spirits [beverages]
330023 whisky
330013 wine

ALOHA SPIRIT IN A BOTTLE® to Koloa Rum Corp. used in association with alcoholic beverages except beers, rum, spirits, prepared alcoholic cocktails; and  to E. REMY MARTIN & C° used in association with alcoholic beverages except beers are examples of marks registered in Int'l Class 33.

Int'l Class 34 – Smokers' Articles
Tobacco and tobacco substitutes; cigarettes and cigars; electronic cigarettes and oral vaporizers for smokers; smokers' articles; matches.

Class 34 has 42 subclasses similar to the following examples:

340012 chewing tobacco
340019 cigarettes containing tobacco substitutes, not for medical purposes
340020 cigarettes
340013 cigars
340039 electronic cigarettes
340040 liquid solutions for use in electronic cigarettes

340033 snuff
340003 tobacco

MOTHERLODE® to M&D Wholesale Distributors, Inc. used in association with cigars, and to Black Ball Corp. used in association with cigarette cases, lighters for smokers, cigarette lighters, cigarette rolling papers and stash boxes are examples of marks registered in Int'l Class 34.

<u>Int'l Class 35 – Advertising and Business</u>
Advertising; business management; business administration; office functions.

Class 35 has 142 subclasses similar to the following examples:

350039 advertising / publicity
350104 production of advertising films
350015 book-keeping / accounting
350001 business management assistance
350017 business auditing
350061 computerized file management
50063 economic forecasting
350031 market studies
350106 marketing
350013 office machines and equipment rental*
350040 radio advertising
350073 tax preparation
350107 telemarketing services
350044 television advertising

WORRY-FREE AUDIT SUPPORT® to H&R Block Digital Tax Solutions, LLC used in association with tax and taxation advice, information and consultancy services, income tax consultation and preparation services featuring tax audit representation services; and to HPT TA Properties Trust used in association with retail store services featuring general merchandise, gasoline and diesel fuel, vending in the field of food, toiletries, electronics and truck maintenance supplies are examples of marks registered in Int'l Class 35.

<u>Int'l Class 36 – Insurance and Financial</u>
Insurance; financial affairs; monetary affairs; real estate affairs.

Class 36 has 187 subclasses similar to the following examples:

360001 accident insurance underwriting
360035 rental of apartments
360052 art appraisal
360013 banking
360005 brokerage
360006 credit bureau services
360058 electronic funds transfer
360030 financial management
360046 financial analysis
360038 health insurance underwriting
360010 insurance brokerage
360044 life insurance underwriting
360040 mortgage banking
360016 mutual funds
360072 online banking
360007 real estate agency services
360110 stock brokerage services

CAREMATTERS® to Nationwide Mutual Insurance Company used in association with insurance administration in the field of life insurance and long-term care insurance, insurance brokerage in the field of life insurance and long-term care insurance, insurance services, namely, underwriting life insurance and long-term care insurance; and the "Hippo" design mark to Virginia Commercial Finance, Inc. used in association with financial services, namely, moneylending services for medical professionals and medical practices are examples of marks registered in Int'l Class 36.

Int'l Class 37 – Building Construction and Repair

Building construction; repair; installation services.

Class 37 has 134 subclasses similar to the following examples:

370008 airplane maintenance and repair
370005 asphalting
370016 burglar alarm installation and repair
370009 cleaning of buildings [interior]
370112 cleaning of buildings [exterior surface]
370029 construction
370036 demolition of buildings
370038 disinfecting
370114 drilling of wells
370133 drilling of deep oil or gas wells
370035 kitchen equipment installation
370058 machinery installation, maintenance and repair
370006 motor vehicle maintenance and repair
370071 plumbing
370109 road paving
370122 roofing services
370021 shipbuilding
370067 upholstering
370055 vehicle washing
370083 vehicle service stations [refueling and maintenance]
370057 washing

ANCHOR TECHNOLOGIES® to Anchor Technologies, Inc. used in association with cyber security consulting and integration services, namely, advisory cyber security services in the nature of advisory services related to installing, maintaining and repairing of cyber security hardware for others, and integration of cyber security networks; and the "Skye" logo to Hintz Holding used in association with aircraft engine repair and maintenance, aircraft fueling services, aircraft maintenance and repair services, aircraft maintenance or repair, aircraft repair and maintenance, fueling services for aircraft, information with relation to aircraft construction, repair and maintenance, outer and inner cleaning of aircraft, repair and maintenance of aircraft, repair, maintenance and modification of aircraft, repair, maintenance and modification of aircraft engines are examples of marks registered in Int'l Class 37.

Int'l Class 38 – Telecommunications
Telecommunications.

Class 38 has 43 subclasses similar to the following examples:

380044 providing access to databases
380021 cable television broadcasting
380010 communications by telephone
380022 communications by cellular phones
380030 communications by fibre / fiber optic networks
380043 providing internet chatrooms
380012 news agency services
380003 radio broadcasting
380035 satellite transmission
380039 teleconferencing services
380009 telephone services
380005 television broadcasting
380025 transmission of electronic mail
380053 video-on-demand transmission

SMILE YOU'RE ON CRICKET WIRELESS® to AT&T Intellectual Property II, L.P. used in association with telecommunication services, namely, wireless telephone services; telecommunications services, namely, local, long distance and international transmission of voice, data, text, video, advertising, gaming and graphics by means of telephone, wireless and handheld and PDA devices and the internet, wireless communication services, namely, wireless mobile telephone calling, electronic messaging and data transmission service plans; and the InstaWatch logo to Wal-Mart Stores, Inc. used in association with streaming of video and audiovisual content on the internet; video-on-demand and audio-on-demand transmission service are examples of marks registered in Int'l Class 38.

Int'l Class 39 – Transportation and Storage
Transport; packaging and storage of goods; travel arrangement.

Class 39 has 108 subclasses similar to the following examples:

390004 air transport
390102 aircraft rental
390006 ambulance transport
390062 armoured-car transport / armored-car transport
390049 boat transport
390100 bottling services
390010 bus transport
390008 car rental
390033 car parking
390074 chauffeur services
390075 courier services [messages or merchandise]
390027 delivery of goods
390090 distribution of energy
390031 electricity distribution
390038 freight [shipping of goods]
390014 hauling
390095 launching of satellites for others
390022 packaging of goods
390020 parcel delivery
390018 railway transport
390028 storage of goods
390058 taxi transport
390048 transport
390003 water supplying

WHITE GLOVE SERVICES® to FedEx Custom Critical, Inc. used in association with transportation of goods of others by truck; and to The Junk Truck, LLC used in association with junk, trash and debris removal are examples of marks registered in Int'l Class 39.

<u>Int'l Class 40 – Treatment of Materials</u>
Treatment of materials.

Class 40 has 120 subclasses similar to the following examples:

400003 air purification
400081 air deodorizing / deodorising
400082 air freshening
400128 beer brewing for others
400049 bookbinding
400036 cloth waterproofing / fabric waterproofing
400037 cloth fireproofing / fabric fireproofing / textile fireproofing
400053 custom tailoring
400102 services of a dental technician
400103 production of energy
400066 food and drink preservation
400084 framing of works of art
400062 glass-blowing
400085 gold plating
400006 paper finishing
400015 pottery firing / firing pottery
400091 processing of oil
400093 refining services
400087 material treatment information
400097 waste treatment [transformation]

PATRIOT ERECTORS® to Patriot Erectors, LLC used in association with steel erecting and construction of buildings, canopies, and bridges; and to PPC Industries, Inc. used in association with catheter assembly and subassembly services for others; custom manufacture of medical and catheter tubing and catheters for others are examples of marks registered in Int'l Class 40.

Int'l Class 41 – Education and Entertainment

Education; providing of training; entertainment; sporting and cultural activities.

Class 41 has 120 subclasses similar to the following examples:

410002 academies [education]
410003 amusement park services
410042 providing casino facilities [gambling]
410057 cinema presentations / movie theatre presentations
410011 correspondence courses
410004 entertainment services
410020 film production, other than advertising films
410094 game services provided online from a computer network
410192 language interpreter services
410196 production of music
410103 news reporters services
410101 photography
410056 presentation of live performances
410024 publication of books
410014 providing recreation facilities
410017 teaching / educational services / instruction services
410031 television entertainment

MUSIC CITY WALK OF FAME® to Nashville Convention & Visitors Bureau used in association with recreational park services featuring space dedicated to honoring those who make, create, record, perform, and present music of every genre across the world; and the Mickey Mouse conductor arrangement to Disney Enterprises, Inc. used in association with arranging and conducting of exhibitions for entertainment purposes, archive library and archive museum services are examples of marks registered in Int'l Class 41.

Int'l Class 42 – Computer and Scientific

Scientific and technological services and research and design relating thereto; industrial analysis and industrial research services; design and development of computer hardware and software.

Class 42 has 111 subclasses similar to the following examples:

420008 analysis for oil-field exploitation
420011 architectural services
420190 biological research
420007 chemical analysis
420031 chemical research
420090 computer programming
420199 creating and maintaining web sites for others
420064 engineering
420049 industrial design
420221 information technology [IT] consultancy
420101 mechanical research
420257 medical research
420095 oil prospecting
420042 oil-well testing
420157 quality control
420161 research and development of new products for others
420217 scientific laboratory services
420222 scientific research
420193 surveying
420058 material testing
420216 water analysis
420234 weather forecasting

METACLOUD® to Cisco Technology, Inc. used in association with infrastructure as a service (IAAS) services featuring software for managing, operating, monitoring, troubleshooting and configuring private cloud computer networks, managing network storage, and for deploying and installing software applications over networks; technical support services, namely, remote infrastructure management services for monitoring, administration and management of private cloud computing IT and application systems, technical support services, namely, troubleshooting in the nature of diagnosing computer software problems; consulting in the field of computer networking technology; consulting in the field of cloud computing; updating and maintaining cloud- based computer software through patches and online updates; and ISOCLEAN SERVICES to Chevron Intellectual Property LLC used in association with technical consultation in the field of fluid conditioning, namely, analyzing and monitoring lubricants, coolants and fuels to facilitate the operation of industrial machinery are examples of marks registered in Int'l Class 42.

Int'l Class 43 – Hotels and Restaurants
Services for providing food and drink; temporary accommodation.

Class 43 has 37 subclasses similar to the following examples:

430004 accommodation bureau services [hotels, boarding houses]
430138 bar services
430134 boarding for animals
430010 food and drink catering
430073 hotel services
430183 motel services
430102 restaurant services

SHORE LEAVE® to HCJ Hospitality, LLC used in association with Bar services and restaurant services, and the Hotel Baxter image to Baxter Main, LLC used in association with technical consultation in the field of fluid conditioning, namely, analyzing and monitoring lubricants, coolants and fuels to facilitate the operation of industrial machinery are examples of marks registered in Int'l Class 43.

Int'l Class 44 – Medical, Beauty and Agriculture
Medical services; veterinary services; hygienic and beauty care for human beings or animals; agriculture, horticulture and forestry services.

Class 44 has 76 subclasses similar to the following examples:

440115 aerial and surface spreading of fertilizers and other agricultural chemicals / aerial and surface spreading of fertilisers and other agricultural chemicals
440131 animal grooming
440020 beauty salon services
440032 chiropractic
440113 dentistry services
440060 health care
440148 lawn care
440021 medical clinic services
440114 nursing home services
440092 opticians' services
440214 orthodontic services
440211 speech therapy

DISCOVER YOU SMILE® to Seabreeze Orthodontics, PA used in association with dentist services and orthodontic services, and to V.N.A. Corporation used in association with home health care services, skilled nursing care, rehabilitation patient care services, physical therapy, occupational therapy services, speech therapy, respiratory therapy services, telemedicine and telehealth services, mental health services, consulting services in the fields of health and nutrition, medical social work services, health care services, namely, providing home health aid services are examples of marks registered in Int'l Class 44.

<u>Int'l Class 45 – Personal and Legal</u>

Legal services; security services for the physical protection of tangible property and individuals; personal and social services rendered by others to meet the needs of individuals.

Class 45 has 67 subclasses similar to the following examples:

450193 adoption agency services
450195 babysitting
450179 fire-fighting

450099 guard services
450206 intellectual property consultancy
450211 litigation services
450213 registration of domain names [legal services]
450231 conducting religious ceremonies

PLAY, ADOPT, LEARN AND GROW® to Annenberg Legacy at Playa Vista LLC used in association with education and entertainment services, namely, conducting seminars and programs in the field of animal health, animal care, animal training, animal behavior, animal history, animal rescue and animal stories, museum services; and to McDivitt Law Firm, P.C. used in association with legal services are examples of marks registered in Int'l Class 45.

Registration of Trademarks in More than One Class

Trademarks may be registered in more than one class, and such classes may include both classes for goods and classes for services as well. Of course, ultimate registration in each of the classes depends upon active use of a good or service in commerce falling within that class. A specimen of use must be submitted to the USPTO demonstrating this actual use in each of the classes. Additionally, payment of the registration fee is effective for each of the classes through which the applicant is seeking registration. Also, failure to continue distribution of goods or services in a respective class will cause the registration in that class to become abandoned. Furthermore, the additional registrations may be filed at the same time in the application for registration or additional applications for registration may be filed in the event it is later decided to register the mark in a particular class.

For example, earlier on the COKE® trademark was registered in Class 06 (containers made of metal/tin), Class 08 (non-mechanical can/bottle opener), Class 11 (electric coolers in the nature of refrigeration units), Class 14 (jewelry), Class 16 (writing instruments and writing pads), Class 25 (clothing) while registrations in Class 9 (radios, etc.), Class 18 (umbrellas, etc.), Class 20 (chairs, cushions, etc.), Class 21 (dishware, etc.), Class 24 (linens, towels, etc.), Class 26 (belt buckle and badges), Class 27 (wall hangings, rugs and placemats), Class 28 (sporting equipment), and Class 34 (matches, lighters and ashtrays) were eventually cancelled. Subsequently, the Coke trademark was registered in Class 21 in association with salt/pepper shakers, toothpick dispensers and napkin dispensers and Class 25 in association with footwear both of which are still active. However, subsequent registrations of the Coke trademark in Class 09 in association with kitchen timers has been allowed to lapse.

CHAPTER 4: What's in a Name

Categories of Marks

Marks have a relative strength that primarily helps to decide how easily protectable they may be. Indeed, some categories of marks may not be protectable at all except in certain limited circumstances or may not continue to be protectable depending upon their categorization. Courts have four categories of marks in determining their degree of strength and protection, which, according to Chapter 7, will have a bearing on whether a likelihood of confusion exists in comparison to an allegedly infringing mark. The following are the categories of marks:

Generic – The name commonly used by many companies for a certain goods or service. Generic names can never receive trademark protection since that would be tantamount to granting a monopoly to that good or service to a registrant.

Descriptive – Descriptive marks directly describe as opposed to suggesting some characteristic, quality, purpose, or component of the good or service. Generally, descriptive marks cannot be registered unless or until they are deemed to have acquired distinctiveness.

Suggestive – A mark that subtly suggests something about the good or service. Suggestive marks are subject to trademark protection.

Arbitrary/Fanciful – A mark that bears little or no relationship to a good or service. Arbitrary and fanciful marks are subject to trademark protection.

The remainder of this Chapter goes deeper into a discussion of these categories of marks.

Generic Marks

Generic terms are the common name typically associated with a product or good manufactured or sold by a company or a service provided by the company. Examples of generic marks include beer, bicycle or cleaning. Generic marks that relate directly to a good or service cannot be trademarked.

Marks that are otherwise generic but are used in association with a class of goods or services that are unrelated to the class of good or service that the generic name refers to may be trademarked. *E.g.*, APPLE® used in association with Class 09 telecommunications devices, and TREES® used in association with certain Class 05 pharmaceutical and veterinary preparations having medicinal herbs have been registered as trademarks. Examples of marks that have been found to be generic include CONSUMER ELECTRONICS and are not subject to trademark protection, notwithstanding whether they have achieved secondary meaning in association with the product or not.

Also, trademarks can become generic or "genericized" if left unprotected by the owner allowing the public to come to associate the name with the good or service. *E.g.*, CELLOPHANE, DRY ICE, ZIPPER and ASPIRIN are marks that have become generic. Certain trademarks have been under the threat of becoming generic until an active stance was taken by the owner of the mark to protect them from becoming generic including, for example, BUBBLE WRAP®, VELCRO®, LEGO®, XEROX® and the Wavy Lines design trademark illustrated here.

Courts typically become the final arbiter in determining whether a mark is or has become generic. This is one of the defenses in a trademark infringement action that quite often is raised. Factors the court can look to in making this determination of whether a mark is or has become generic include dictionary definitions to determine whether the term is related to the goods or services in question; use of the term by the trademark registrant in describing the goods or services; use of the term by others in referring to similar goods or services; use of the term in publications in association with similar goods or services; extent of use of other terms in describing similar goods or services; and survey evidence (surveys are discussed in more detail in Chapter 8).

Descriptive Marks

Descriptive marks are expressive types of marks that generally convey an immediate idea concerning the ingredients, qualities or characteristics of the goods or services. Subject matter that has been deemed to be descriptive includes marks conveying the purpose, function, use, size, merit, quantity, or capacity of a product, for example; class of intended purchasers of the good or service, and the effect the good or service has upon the user.

Examples of marks that have been deemed to be descriptive include LITE when used in association with beer; PARK 'N FLY used in association with airport parking and transport services; HONEY-BAKED used in associated with a ham, in particular, the way the ham is prepared; and ULTIMATE BIKE RACK used in association with a bike rack. Thus, in order to determine whether a mark is descriptive it is necessary to know the class and possibly description of goods or services with which the mark is used in association with.

Acquired Distinctiveness or Secondary Meaning

Descriptive marks can be subject to trademark protection if acquired distinctiveness or "secondary meaning" is established for the mark—*i.e.*, if it can be shown that the mark has come to be associated with a certain producer or supplier of goods or services. Typically, it takes some period of use of the mark in sales or advertising to establish secondary meaning (usually five years of substantially exclusive and continuous use). Indeed, a presumption of distinctiveness can be demonstrated to the USPTO by submitting proof that the use of the mark on goods or services in commerce was "substantially exclusive and continuous" for the past five years. Such proof may be by way of an affidavit, for example, but typically requires other evidentiary proof as well.

For example, HOLIDAY INN®, EXTRA STRENGTH PAIN RELIEVER® and TENDER VITTLES® have been shown to have established secondary meaning in association with the hotelier, a pharmaceutical company's EXCEDRIN® product, and a pet food supplier, respectively. In response to an Office Action rejection over the course of prosecution of a mark alleging distinctiveness, the following types of evidence, typically collectively, may be used to establish a showing of secondary meaning:

1) *Prior Registrations* – A claim of ownership of one or more active prior registrations on the Principal Register of the same mark for goods or services that are sufficiently similar to those identified in the pending application.
2) *Five Years' Use* – A verified statement that the mark has become distinctive of the applicant's goods or services by reason of the applicant's substantially exclusive and continuous use of the mark in commerce for the five years before the date on which the claim of distinctiveness is made.
3) *Other Evidence* – Other appropriate evidence of acquired distinctiveness including verified statements, depositions, or other appropriate evidence showing (i) duration of use, (ii) extent of use, and (iii) nature of the use in commerce; advertising expenditures in connection therewith (identifying types of media and attaching typical advertisements); and verified statements, letters or statements from the trade or public, or both, or other appropriate evidence of distinctiveness.

Deceptively Misdescriptive

The trademark statutes do not allow a deceptive mark to be registered. The following is the test that has been established for deceptiveness:

- The term is misdescriptive of the character, quality, function, composition or use of the goods.
- Prospective purchasers are likely to believe that the misdescription actually describes the goods.
- The misdescription is likely to affect the purchaser's decision to purchase the goods or services.

For example, WHITE JASMINE falsely indicated goods contained white tea, which was the material factor in a consumer's purchasing decision and not subject to registration. It was determined that this mark was deceptively misdescriptive since the product did not have white tea.

Many misdescriptive marks are not necessarily considered deceptive, including, for example, GLASS WAX®, which contained no wax, but it was demonstrated that consumers did not purchase the product because it had wax.

Geographic deceptive misdescriptive marks are not subject to protection either. Some examples of geographic misdescriptive marks that are deceptive include:

- "AMERICA" or "AMERICAN" used with goods or services that are not from the United States and such use is intended to be deceptive.
- DURANGO chewing tobacco not grown in Durango, Mexico.

Personal Names

Personal names include the use of a merchant's name in a mark that is descriptive. Indeed, surnames are deemed to have a nontrademark meaning unless there is a showing of acquired distinctiveness or secondary meaning.

For a personal name to be treated to be a mark in the descriptive sense, it must first be determined that the name is "primarily merely a surname." While "Bird" is used as a surname, it also connotes to those feathered creatures of flight surrounding us. Therefore, "Bird" would not be considered "primarily merely a surname."

However, marks that are determined to be "primarily merely a surname" may be shown to have acquired distinctiveness or secondary meaning. For Example, the surname included in MRS. SASSARDS used in association with preserves, namely, preserved fruit and vegetables, jams, jellies, pickled fruits, and pickled vegetables, preserved vegetables, namely, preserved Jerusalem artichokes was found to have acquired distinctiveness upon a showing the surname was used in association with such goods since 1917. Dorothea Benton Franks novel entitled *Plantation* (A Low Country Tale) (published July 1, 2001) even describes scooping up a spoon of Mrs. Sassard's artichoke relish to eat with her meat, although a showing of five years would have merely been sufficient.

Geographic Terms

Use of geographic location in a mark is considered descriptive. Geographic locations in and of themselves are deemed to have a nontrademark meaning.

In order to be descriptive, marks including a geographic location must be sourced from that location so as not to be misdescriptive. Similar to personal names, however, marks having a geographic location must be "primarily geographically descriptive." These locations are not considered "primarily geographically descriptive" if the place is not well-known, the location also constitutes a surname, or the location does not impart information as to the source of the goods (*e.g.*, NANTUCKET® for shirts not necessarily sourced from there but conveying distinctiveness concerning where the shirts are suitable to be worn).

However, again marks that are considered "primarily geographically descriptive" may only be subject to trademark registration upon a showing of acquired distinctiveness and, in the particular case of the these geographically descriptive marks, are not deceptive.

Suggestive Marks

Suggestive marks identify the source of the goods or services immediately upon use and are subject to trademark protection without the need to establish secondary meaning. While suggestive marks still suggest something about the goods or services, some degree of imagination, thought, and perception is needed to reach a conclusion of the connection in order for the mark not to be considered to be descriptive. A declaration by the USPTO that a mark is suggestive serves as *prima facie* evidence that a mark is not merely descriptive thus not requiring a showing of acquired distinctiveness.

Examples of suggestive marks include ACOUSTIC RESEARCH® used in association with home speakers, GREYHOUND® for bus transportation, Q-TIPS® for cotton tipped swabs, and UNCOLA® the noncola soft drink. In the case of GREYHOUND®, the dogs are known to be sleek and fast, and while these traits may be recognized in a bus, some degree of thought is still needed to make the association. This is in contrast to QUICK STOP, for example, which is merely descriptive of a convenience store that one can stop in to for quick service. While Kuwait Petroleum Company has not attempted registration of the Q8 mark, it would likely be considered by the Office to be a suggestive term because the immediate connation is not to Kuwait and does not necessarily represent a deceptively misdescriptive geographic representation as to the source of products. Suggestive marks do run a risk of becoming generic if proactive control of the use of the mark is not assumed by the registrant to prevent this. At times, the extent of use of a suggestive mark may be such that it promulgates the mark to be more descriptive of the associated goods or services.

Arbitrary and Fanciful Marks

Arbitrary marks are common words that are applied to goods or services in a non-descriptive way. Arbitrary marks are words that have a particular dictionary defined significance, but instead of signifying that defined thing, the mark signifies goods or services that are entirely different than the defined term. Examples of arbitrary marks include CAMELS® in association with cigarettes; APPLE® representative of computers, smart phones, software and retail services; and the Ralph Loren Polo Player image used in association with fragrances.

Fanciful marks are coined or made-up terms with no defined meaning at all. The fanciful mark only becomes meaningful when used in association with the related goods or services. Examples of fanciful marks that gained recognition of goods or services include KODAK®, CLOROX®, EXXON®, XEROX®, ROLEX® and PEPSI®. Fanciful marks do require policing to ensure use by others does not cause the mark to eventually become generic (see generic marks above).

Strength or Distinctiveness of a Mark

In many jurisdictions, the strength or distinctiveness of a mark is considered to be one of the "paramount" factors in determining whether there is a likelihood of confusion in association with the mark (all factors considered are discussed in more detail in Chapter 7).[1] Courts have determined that a mark that is merely descriptive is considered to be weak and cannot be accorded trademark protection without proof of secondary

Spectrum of Distinctiveness		
← **Strong Marks**		**Weak Marks →**
Inherently Distinctive Marks	**Non-Inherently Distinctive Marks**	**Marks Lacking any Distinctiveness**
Acquired Distinctiveness not Required	Acquired Distinctiveness Required	Not at all Subject to Registration
Inherently Distinctive Marks may be Registered	May only be Registered upon a showing of Distinctiveness.	Not Entitled to Registration
Arbitrary Marks **Fanciful Marks** **Suggestive Marks**	**Merely Descriptive Marks** **Personal Name Marks** **Primariy Geographic Descriptive Marks**	**Generic Marks**

1 *Pizzeria Uno Corp. v. Temple*, 747 F.2d 1522, 1527 (4th Cir., 1984).

meaning, while a mark that is either suggestive or arbitrary is strong and presumptively valid. Thus, the spectrum of strength, as exhibited in the included table, is of particular importance in a determining whether there is a likelihood of confusion that exists between marks.

Nicknames and Abbreviations of Trademarks

The public use doctrine is a limited scope court precedent that allows trademark owners to stake a claim to nicknames or abbreviations that the public has come to associate with the mark. For example, at first COKE was adopted as a nickname for COCA-COLA, but now has become a registered mark because of its rampant use by the company. Similarly, BUD was adopted by consumers as a nickname for BUDWEISER. Courts embrace the concept since an abbreviation or nickname typically adds distinctiveness to the owner's mark. However, the Fourth Circuit has made clear that the concept does not work the other way around—*i.e.*, expanding the protective scope of a trademark to include a full-name interpretation of an abbreviation or nickname that has been registered.[2]

Fair Use

Statutory Fair Use

The Lanham Act is supportive of the concept of fair use. Fair use of a person's individual name in a business. Furthermore, fair use protects the use of a geographic term in describing the geographic origin of goods. 15 U.S.C. § 1115(b)(4). Even in the circumstances where a surname or geographic name has acquired secondary meaning and becomes a registered trademark for the user, another merchant may still use his same surname or geographic location in a non-trademark sense—*e.g.*, by identifying the persons name or geographic location in associated print.

---

[2] *George & Co. LLC v. Imagination Entertainment Ltd.*, 575 F.3d 383, 403-4 (4th Cir., 2009) ("Peanut Butter & Jelly" does not make "PB & J" more distinctive and similarly "Bacon, Lettuce, and Tomato" does not make "BLT" more distinctive).

Indeed, asserting statutory fair use as a defense often turns on whether the defendant uses the trademark too prominently on its product or in its advertising.

Nominative Fair Use

Nominative fair use centers around the descriptive use of a registered trademark to describe or identify the associated goods or services. The Ninth Circuit has determined that three criteria must be met to successfully assert a nominative fair use: (i) the product or service in question must be one that is not readily identifiable without the use of the trademark; (2) only so much of the mark or marks may be used as is reasonably necessary to identify the product or service; and (3) the use must do nothing that would, in conjunction with the mark, suggest sponsorship or endorsement of the defendant's goods or services by the trademark holder.

CHAPTER 5: Principal versus Supplemental Registers

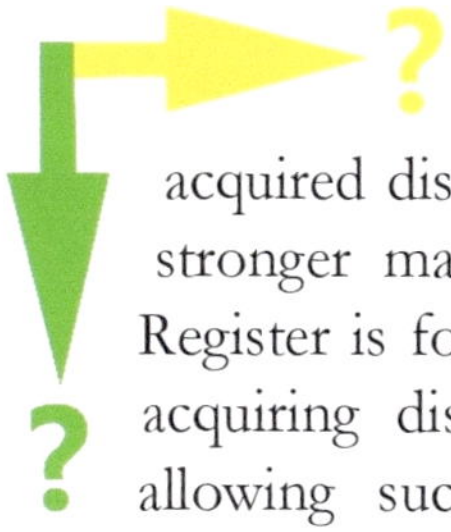

There are two types of registers in the United States depending upon the category and the status of the mark. The Principal Register is for arbitrary/fanciful, suggestive or descriptive marks that have acquired distinctiveness or secondary meaning, clearly the stronger marks of the two registers. The Supplemental Register is for descriptive marks that are in the process of acquiring distinctiveness or secondary meaning perhaps allowing such marks to be eventually registered as a trademark and then moving to the Principal Register.

Five years of substantially exclusive and continuous use of the mark in commerce in association with the goods and/or services for which the mark is being used in association with and being registered for is required to allow the mark to presumptively acquire secondary meaning and allowed to be moved to the Principal Register.

Advantages of the Principal Register

The advantages of registration on the Principal Register include the following:

- *Prima facie* evidence of validity of the registered mark demonstrating the exclusive right to use the mark in commerce in connection with the goods and/or services of the trademark (*prima facie* evidence can only be overturned with rebuttal evidence introduced by the opposing party).
- *Prima facie* evidence of continued use since the date of application for registration of the mark.
- Incontestability of the trademark after five years of continuous use, which precludes cancellation on the basis of prior use or descriptiveness.

- Constructive notice of ownership of the mark by registrant.
- Generally, nationwide rights.
- Right to bring suit in federal court under federal question jurisdiction (*i.e.*, diversity of citizenship with plaintiff and defendant(s) residing or incorporated in separate states and greater than $75,000 amount in controversy not required).
- Subject to statutory remedies including mandatory treble damages.
- Criminal penalties are applied in counterfeit cases.
- Upon depositing the registration with customs, any goods bearing the trademark may not be imported into the United States.
- Paris Convention rights including the right to register abroad within six months of the application for registration in the United, States, and priority rights on foreign filings dating back to the date of filing in the United States.
- Trademarks on the Principal Register can and should be marked with an ® instead of a ™ symbol to provide constructive notice of registration of the mark.

The presumptions accorded to trademarks registered on the Principal Register do not apply to registrations on the Supplemental Register, because the mark on the Supplemental Register is only considered capable of becoming a trademark, but an actual determination concerning registration has not been accorded to the Supplemental Register marks.

Advantages of the Supplemental Register

While not accorded the advantages of a trademark that has been registered on the Principal Register, the Supplemental Register does provide the following advantages over not doing any registration at all:

- Deterrence against use or registration of the mark by others while it is acquiring distinctiveness.

- Not subject to the same rights as marks on the Principal Register since marks on the Supplemental Register are considered only capable of becoming a trademark. *I.e.*, marks are not considered a trademark while on the Supplemental Register.
- Even though marks on the supplemental register are not formally considered to be trademarks, they may be marked with the ®.
- Registrants are allowed to pursue registration of the mark in a foreign country/jurisdiction.
- Registrants may bring suit in federal court against another's use of the mark in association with the goods or services for which the mark is attempting to become distinctive.

Once a mark on the Supplemental Register has acquired distinctiveness—typically based upon five years of exclusive and substantially continuous use by the owner of the mark. However, marks do not become automatically transferred to the Principal Registe. Rather, an application for registration of the mark must be filed with the USPTO for consideration of whether to allow the mark to be registered as a trademark on the Principal Register. The procedure for preparing and filing an application for registration of a mark is provided in Chapter 6.

State Registration of Trademarks

Trademarks may be registered under state law. If the owner of the mark is only considering use in a particular state, then this option may be considered. Typically, the costs associated with registration of a mark in a state are lower than those for a federal registration. However, registration in the state will only provide regional coverage in that state and will not necessarily extend to similar marks that may then be registered. While the registrant's state use will remain protected, that use may never be extended outside of the state if a mark that is deemed similar to that registered in the state achieves federal registration.

State registrations of a mark are typically only limited by marks or trade names used in that state that would be deemed confusingly similar to such a mark or trade name. Many states have trademark databases of trademarks that have been registered in that state that may be searched in an attempt to see if there are any that may be deemed confusingly similar. However, the registrant's search should also include the business registration database for the state to identify any existing trade names that may be deemed confusingly similar. Finally, the applicant should consider also searching the USPTO Trademark Electronic Search System (TESS) to identify any marks that are still active that could be deemed confusingly similar to the mark.

Furthermore, unlike the federal registration of marks, many states require the mark to be in actual use. *I.e.*, a bona fide intent-to-use a mark may not serve as a basis for registering the mark in the state.

State registrations are still based upon class or classes of use and may have a fee of anywhere from $25 to $75 per class depending on the state.

CHAPTER 6: Federal Registration of Trademarks

Marks are registered in the United States by filing an application for registration of the mark with the USPTO. The information in the application will vary depending upon the type of application form selected. The following three application forms and their requirements for information are provided here:

(1) TEAS Plus

- Requires an email address to be provided and an agreement to correspond by email with the USPTO concerning the application.
- Additional application-related submissions must be filed online including responses to office actions.
- Must select a goods or services listing from the already identified USPTO Trademark Identification (ID) Manual, and the selection must accurately identify the goods or services with which the mark is associated.
- Additional information required if applicable including whether the same mark has already been registered in the USPTO by the applicant, the mark includes a color, the mark includes a design or stylized font, the mark includes non-English words, the mark includes non-Latin characters, the mark includes the name or portrait of a living person, or the mark is currently in use and the specific geographic area needs to be limited with other concurrent users identified.
- At the time of publication, the filing fee for TEAS Plus is $225 per class of goods or services for which the mark is being registered.

(2) TEAS RF

- Requires an email address to be provided and an an agreement to correspond by email with the USPTO concerning the application.
- Additional application-related submissions must be filed online including responses to office actions.
- No additional information needs to be provided with the application.
- At the time of publication, the filing fee for TEAS RF is $275 per class of goods or services for which the mark is being registered.

(3) TEAS Regular

- No particular requirements.
- The application need not be submitted electronically to the USPTO.
- At the time of publication, the filing fee for TEAS Regular is $400 per class of goods or services for which the mark is being registered.

The TEAS Plus application has the most onerous requirements given the additional information that must be filed and the limitation on the goods or services listing that can be selected but is the lowest in cost to file with the USPTO.

TEAS RF mostly allows the applicant to get around the limiting requirements of the goods or services listing must be found in the Trademark ID Manual that accurately identifies the goods or services for which the mark is being registered in association with. If the applicant's goods or services are not closely related to the available listings in TEAS Plus, then a TEAS RF or a TEAS Regular application allows the applicant to develop their own goods or services listing

The TEAS Regular application allows the applicant to proceed with an application for registration if they have no desire to communicate electronically with the USPTO concerning the application. Certainly, if information is lacking concerning the additional information required in the TEAS Plus application, then either the TEAS RF or TEAS Regular application should be filed to at least accord the mark with a filing date that allows an earlier priority date.

Outline for Process of Application for Registration of a Mark in Use in Commerce

(1) Prepare and file application for registration that includes a statement of use and a specimen of use for each class being registered.

(2) Examination (otherwise known as trademark prosecution) by the United States Patent and Trademark Office to make the following determinations:

- The mark is a mark or is capable of becoming a mark (*e.g.*, mark is not merely descriptive, geographically misdescriptive or deceptive, primarily merely a surname, etc.);
- The mark is not likely to be confused with a trademark that has been previously registered; and
- Registration of the mark is not proscribed by other section 2 prohibitions.

(3) Upon approval that the mark conforms to the statutory requirements identified above, the mark is submitted for publication for a period of thirty days where a third party has an opportunity to file an opposition against the mark or seek an extension-of-time to file an opposition.

(4) USPTO issues Notice of Allowance following expiration of the opposition period (assuming no opposition has been filed).

(5) Issuance of registration certificate (about two to four months following the close of the opposition period).

Outline for Process of Application for Registration of a Bona Fide Intention to Use Mark

(1) Prepare and file application for registration that includes a declaration of bona fide intention to use the mark in commerce on the specified goods and/or services.

(2) Examination (otherwise known as trademark prosecution) by the USPTO using the same criteria as that identified for a mark in use in commerce.
(3) Upon approval that the mark conforms to the statutory requirements, the mark is submitted for publication for a period of thirty days where a third party has an opportunity to file an opposition against the mark or seek an extension-of-time to file an opposition.
(4) USPTO issues Notice of Allowance following expiration of the opposition period.
(5) Registrant must submit a statement of use along with a specimen of use within six months of the Notice of Allowance, which may be extended for six-month periods up to five times allowing a period of thirty-six months over which to demonstrate actual use.
(6) Issuance of registration certificate (about two months following verification of the specimen of use by the USPTO).

Application for Registration of a Mark

The sections that follow identifies the information to be include in the application for registration of a mark.

Identify Applicant

The general requirement is that the applicant or applicants must be filed by the owner(s) of the mark, and, in the case of an intent-to-use application, the applicant is the person or organization that is entitled to use the mark in commerce. Applicants may include any one or combination of the following:

- Individual – include county of citizenship.
- Individual with an assumed name designation – include individual's name followed by the named designation, *e.g.*, d.b.a., a.k.a., *etc.*
- Corporations, partnerships, joint ventures, unions and other organizations – include state of registration of organization.

- Nations, states, municipalities and other types of bodies operating with governmental authorization to apply to register the mark – description of entity is based upon laws of governing body overseeing the applicant.
- Trust, conservatorships and estates – list the name of the trustee, conservator and executor/administrator, respectively, in the stated capacity.

The name of the applicant must be listed in its correct legal form.

Identification and Classification of Goods and Services

An application for registration of the trademark must include a list of the goods and/or services to be used in connection with the mark. The international class number(s) as discussed in Chapter 3 that coordinate with the identified goods or services must be identified.

While applicants may desire to want to attempt to capture as much in the goods or services listing as possible, it should be noted that failure to eventually use such a good or service may cause the registration to become abandoned for non-use. Therefore, the listing of goods or services should fully cover the goods or services currently in use in commerce or those goods or services the applicant has a bona fide intention of using in commerce.

Filing Basis

The filing basis provides the statutory basis for filing the application for registration of the mark. The filing basis that can be selected are:

1) Use of the mark in commerce.[1]
2) Bona fide intention to use the mark in commerce.[2]

---

[1] §1(a) of the Trademark Act.

[2] §1(a) of the Trademark Act.

3) Priority claim based upon an earlier filed foreign application.[3]
4) Ownership of a registration of the mark in the applicant's country of origin.[4]
5) Extension of protection of an international application to the United States.[5]

In an application under (1)-(4) above, the applicant may claim more than one basis (this is not possible under (5) above), but the applicant may not claim use of the mark in commerce and bona fide intention to use the mark in commerce for identical goods in the same application. However, the goods or services in the same class may be delineated among use of the mark in commerce and bona fide intention to use the mark in commerce basis for the varying goods or services. For example, the following notation may be used:

Class 027: (Based on Use in Commerce) carpets, rugs;
(Based on Intent to Use) mats
Class 027: (Based on 44(e)) wallpaper

Basis notations are not required when it is clear that only one basis is selected for that class of goods or services. Of course, specimens of use must be provided for any goods or services to which a §1(a) use of the mark in commerce filing basis applies.

Dates of First Use

In applications for marks based upon use in commerce, the application must include the date of first use anywhere, whether in the United States or elsewhere, and the date of first use in commerce. The date of first use in commerce is the date when goods were first sold or transported, or services were first rendered under the mark in a type of commerce that may be lawfully regulated by the U.S. Congress. The date of first use will always

---

[3] §44(d) of the Trademark Act.
[4] §44(e) of the Trademark Act.
[5] §66(a) of the Trademark Act.

either be earlier than or the same as the date of first use in commerce.

When these dates are indefinite, the applicant should always provide the date that is most definite. Entries such as "at least as early as," "prior to," "before," "on or about" and "in" are acceptable for the record. Dates of first use that provide only the month and date will be interpreted as having a first use on the last day of the specified month.

Specimens of Use

Again, in applications for marks based upon use in commerce, a specimen of use for each class must be provided. Specimens of use are intended to show the manner in which the mark is seen by the public on or in connection with the goods or in the sale or advertising of the services.

Generally, if more than one item of goods or services is specified in a class, it is usually not necessary to provide a specimen of use for each product or service. However, if the range of items for a class is quite broad or contains unrelated articles, the examining attorney may request additional specimen(s) of use be provided.

In an application for marks with a filing basis of a bona fide intention to use, specimens of use are not required at the time the application is filed. However, before a registration of the mark issues, the applicant must file an allegation of use that includes a specimen of use for each class or at least the class where use has commenced.

In applications with goods or services having both a use in commerce basis and a bona fide intention to use in commerce basis, those goods or services having the use in commerce basis must each include a specimen of use with the application, and the specimen(s) of use along with an allegation of use for those having a bona fide intention to use in commerce must be provided before a registration of the mark in association with those goods or services will issue.

If color is a feature of the mark, or if the mark consists solely of color, the specimen of use must show use of the color.

If a trademark is ordinarily applied to the goods or to the containers for goods by means of a label, the label may be submitted as a specimen of use. Shipping or mailing labels may be accepted if they are affixed to the goods or to the containers for the goods and proper trademark usage is shown on the labels. A photograph of a good or container for the goods stamped with the trademark is an acceptable specimen of use. Such a stamp may be by metal imprint, rubber ink stamp or stenciling.

A web page that displays a product may constitute a "display associated with the goods" and submitted as a specimen of use if the web page: (i) contains a picture or textual description of the identified goods, (ii) shows the mark in association with the goods, (iii) provides a means for ordering the identified goods and (iv) displays the mark in a manner that customers will recognize it as a mark.

If materials provided in a package with the goods is merely advertising material, then this is not acceptable as a specimen of use. Furthermore, package inserts that include the mark such as invoices, announcements, order forms, bills of lading, leaflets, brochures, printed advertising material, circulars and press releases are not acceptable specimens of use since they do not show use of the mark <u>on</u> the goods.

<u>Drawing of the Mark</u>

The application must include a clear drawing of the mark except in applications for registration of sound, scent or other non-visual marks. The drawing will be used to reproduce the mark in the registration certificate and is needed to receive a filing date for the application. Submission of a specimen of use showing how the mark is to be used is not an acceptable form of the drawing. *I.e.*, the drawing of the mark is separate and distinct from the requirements of the specimen of use for the mark.

There are two forms of drawings—"standard character drawings" and "special form drawings." Applicants who seek to register, words, letters, numbers or any combination thereof without a claim to font style, size or color must submit a standard character drawing that shows the mark in black on a white background. A standard character mark is appropriate when:

- The application includes a statement that the mark is in standard characters and no claim is made to any particular font style, size or color.
- The mark does not include a design element.
- All letters and words in the mark are depicted in Latin characters.
- All numerals in the mark are depicted in Roman or Arabic numerals.
- The mark includes only common punctuation or diacritical marks.

Special form drawings are required for marks having a two- or three-dimensional design; color; and/or words, letters or numbers or any combination thereof in a particular font style, or size. The drawing should show the mark in black on a white background unless the mark is intended to lay claim to a color. An illustrated rendering of the drawing is most appropriate for a special form drawing. While a photograph of the mark may be acceptable, the photograph must accurately depict the mark and there can be no other matter shown in the photograph that is not part of the mark.

Verification of Application

The averments required in a verification signed by the applicant or attorney representing the applicant (digital signatures in TEAS Plus and TEAS RF applications) must include the following:

- *Truth of Facts Recited* – "to the best of the signatory's knowledge and belief, the facts recited in the application are accurate."
- *Use in Commerce* – for this type of filing basis, the applicant must submit a statement verifying such.

- *Bona Fide Intention to Use in Commerce* – for this type of filing basis, the applicant must submit a verified statement that the applicant has a bona fide intention to use the mark in commerce.
- *Ownership or Entitlement to Use* – applicant believes they are the owner of the mark, and, to the best of the signatory's knowledge or belief, no other person has the right to use the mark in commerce, either in identical form of the mark or in such near resemblance as to be likely to cause confusion or mistake, or to deceive.

Required Filing Fee

In order for the application to be submitted to the USPTO, the filing fee must also be submitted. At the time of publication of this book, the following application fees apply:

- TEAS Plus – $225 per class of goods or services for which the mark is being registered.
- TEAS RF – $275 per class of goods or services for which the mark is being registered.
- TEAS Regular – $400 per class of goods or services for which the mark is being registered.

Section 44 Foreign Applications & Foreign Registrations

A Section 44 basis of filing seeks to register a trademark already filed in a foreign application or existing foreign registration. Such applications may be based on actual use in commerce or a bona fide intention to use the mark in commerce. To be eligible, the applicant's country of origin must be a party to an international agreement with the United States that provides a right of priority or extends reciprocal rights to priority to United States nationals, and the foreign application must be filed in such a country. Generally, the application in the United States must be filed within six months of the application for foreign registration of the trademark in order to receive the filing date of the foreign application as the priority date in the United States.

Description of goods and/or services included in the foreign application may require amendment in order to conform to USPTO requirements and to ensure the description is broad enough to cover the applicant's intended use of bona fide intention to use marks. Additionally, any specimens of use submitted for marks already used in commerce must conform to the U.S. requirements.

Section 66 International Registration Applications

§66(e) filing basis are for applications where the applicant has an international registration through the World Intellectual Property Organization (WIPO), and they desire the rights under that registration to extend to the United States. Generally, registrations under WIPO serve as a place holder for a reduced cost until a decision is made to proceed with registration in the designated country. Many countries may be accorded a designated status under the international registration, each having a reduced cost over what it would otherwise cost to proceed directly with a registration in those countries. If a party chooses not to proceed with registration in all countries, then this approach could save the application money overall. However, even with international registration, the rights in the mark do not accrue until the application actually becomes registered in the designated country.

Using a Trademark

Notice of trademark ownership is important, and failure to provide notice can have significant monetary consequences. The Trademark Act provides that a registrant of a mark registered in the USPTO may provide notice that the mark is registered by displaying with the mark the words "Registered in the U.S. Patent and Trademark Office" or "Reg. U.S. Pat. & Tm. Off." or the use of the letter R enclosed by a circle ® as illustrated here.

®

Providing such information is considered constructive notice and allows the registrant to be awarded damages since the start of infringement of the mark by an unauthorized user of the mark. If, however, the registrant fails to provide notice of registration of the mark, no profits or damages are recoverable under the Lanham Act unless the unauthorized user had actual notice of the registration. At what point in time an unauthorized user gains actual knowledge of the registration is more difficult to prove and, many times, is construed to be the time the registrant brings an action against the unauthorized user of the mark. This can result in a substantial portion of damages not being awarded. So, the registrant should actively work to always provide constructive notice of the registration.

An applicant may delineate the mark while it is awaiting registration in the USPTO—a process which can take as little as less than a year in some cases or possibly longer in the case of an egregious opposition against the registration of the mark—by using a superscript "TM" following the trademark or a superscript "SM" following a service mark. Once your mark becomes registered, the "TM" or "SM" following the mark should be replaced with the "®" symbol. It is illegal to use the "®" symbol or provide other notice of registration for a mark that has not been registered or for those trademarks that have not been renewed. You must renew the registration of your trademark every ten years as long as your use of the trademark in association with the registered service or product continues.

TM

SM

At times, the applicant desires to obtain a broader listing of goods or services for the registration of the mark in a designated class, which allows the goods or services through which you use the registered trademark in association with to evolve within that generally described space as you continue to use the trademark and possibly expand your products or services. However, for goods and services that substantially differ from those in actual use or having a bona fide intention to use at the time of the application, it is typically better to expand the scope of the registration once you have used the new goods or services in commerce or you have a bona fide intention to use such substantially different goods or services within three years of an application for these goods or services. The open-ended approach of a goods or services listing raises the possibility of an argument of abandonment if such goods or services were not used in association with the mark for a certain period of time. Indeed, a presumption of abandonment exists if the substantially different goods or services had not been used in association with the mark for three years.

As mentioned above, continuous use of the trademark in commerce is required to maintain trademark rights. Continued use must be demonstrated to the USPTO following the fifth year of continuous use of the trademark by filing a Section 8 affidavit of use. While not mandatory, a Section 15 affidavit of incontestability within the year following the fifth year of registration to provide the registrant with "incontestable" rights to the trademark is recommended.

Renewal of the registration is required every ten years sometime within the year preceding expiration of the trademark (six-month grace period for renewal does exist). The renewal fee due every ten years for a registered trademark is currently $425 for each class of goods or services for which the mark is registered if the requisite Section 8 (declaration of use and/or excusable non-use) and Section 9 (renewal application) is filed between the 9th and 10th year after registration. A six-month grace period for filing such forms extends beyond the tenth year, but currently requires an additional $200 fee for each class to be included. Nonetheless, the long-term, continued cost of ownership for a registered trademark is not that exorbitant. An affidavit of use must also be filed with the renewal verifying continued use.

Policing Your Trademark

In addition to continued use, policing your trademark is somewhat of a consequence to also maintaining your rights to the trademark. Failure to actively protect the mark can also result in the inability to obtain damages in a subsequent trademark

infringement action and ultimately perhaps even the mark being declared to have acquired genericness (see Chapter 4 concerning the categorization of generic marks) if the use is somewhat rampant and uncontrolled among unauthorized third party users.

Professional watch organizations may be employed to review published marks open for opposition in the USPTO. Additionally, these organizations can perform public searches to identify any potential infringement. These services can be somewhat costly, however.

Another good source for monitoring unauthorized use of your trademarks are the company's own employees who periodically attend trade shows and have communications with distributors and wholesale or retailers with who your company does business. The employees should be instructed to report such uses to their manager or supervisor who then should relay such information to legal for further analysis.

Given today's prevalent use of the Internet, periodic online searches of the mark, perhaps on a quarterly basis, can also potentially identify any infringing use. These periodic searches should also include the Trademark Electronic Search System (TESS) so that potentially conflicting marks can be identified. While prosecution of the mark before the examining attorney is not an *ex parte* process where third parties would be allowed to submit information to the examining attorney for consideration, a third party who believes they may be damaged by the registration has an opportunity to submit a Notice of Opposition to oppose registration of the mark in the event the examining attorney finds the mark allowable and the mark proceeds to publication in the *Official Gazette*. An opponent has 30 days to file a Notice of Opposition, but this period may be extended by up to 150 days upon filing a request through the Electronic System for Trademark

Trials and Appeals (ESTTA). Extensions for an additional 30 days may be granted without reason, while the next 60 days must be supported by good cause or consent of the registrant. The final 60 days can only be granted again with consent of the registrant or a showing of extraordinary circumstances. The Notice of Opposition serves as the complaint in the opposition proceeding and must include the opponent's reasons why registration of the mark should not be granted.

Once a trademark has issued, a Petition for Cancellation may be filed with the ESTTA. Although it should be preferred to identify potentially conflicting marks prior to their publication so that an opposition may be filed, a Petition for Cancellation gives a third party an opportunity to attempt to have the registration of the conflicting mark cancelled if the third party used the same or a confusingly similar mark. While an Opposition is preferred, the Petition for Cancelation still provides an opportunity to address the matter. This approach, however, begins to suffer beyond five years of publication of the mark since the arguments in support of cancellation are more limited. Suh arguments after this five-year period include the mark has become a generic name for the goods or services, the mark is functional, the mark has been abandoned, registration of the mark obtained fraudulently or registered contrary to statutory provisions of the act.

Cease and Desist Letter

At times, it may become apparent that a third party has merely adopted the trademark for use without attempting to register the mark in the USPTO. If such a use is deemed to be confusingly similar with the intended use of the trademark as registered by the registrant, then the third party should be advised to discontinue use of the mark. This is typically done through a "cease and desist" letter whereby the third party is advised of the registrant's rights in the trademark, and a warning that they should immediately stop their illegal use of the trademark. An attorney should draft and send such a letter on the registrant's behalf.

Declaratory Judgment Action

At times, special circumstances may dictate an alternative approach. Cease and desist letters are considered a showing that an actual controversy exists between the parties. An actual controversy provides justification to the third party to file what is known as a declaratory judgment action in federal court. Such an action provides the third party with a jurisdictional basis to sue the registrant in an effort to establish that they are not liable for infringement of the registered mark. Thus, the potential infringer is given the choice of jurisdiction for where the lawsuit can be filed, which can be removed from the jurisdiction where the registrant normally does business. A declaratory judgment action also provides the alleged infringer with certain procedural advantages in the lawsuit as well. Therefore, an analysis should be done prior to sending a cease and desist letter to determine whether a declaratory judgment action could ensue based upon who the alleged infringer is. This should also extend to considering who the customers and suppliers of the third party are since they could also commence a declaratory judgment action as well. For example, if any of these parties are bitter rivals of the registrant, then it may be a better approach for the registrant to file a lawsuit in the jurisdiction of their choice. A complaint to commence the lawsuit need not be fully developed, but must simply include enough information to survive a motion to dismiss as well as some other procedural challenges. If the lawsuit later continues to ensue without the third party voluntarily stopping their infringing use of the trademark, then the complaint can always be amended to expand the facts and the claims in the lawsuit.

Certainly, if it is decided to send a cease and desist letter to the alleged infringer, then the registrant may still need to pursue a lawsuit if the alleged infringer either ignores the letter or argues in a response that supports their use of the mark. Certainly, any arguments they provide should be researched and reviewed to determine whether their continued use should be allowed or not.

CHAPTER 7: Likelihood of Confusion

The Lanham Act provides that any person who without consent of the registrant uses in commerce any reproduction, counterfeit, copy or colorable imitation of a registered mark in connection with the sale, offering for sale, distribution or advertising of goods or services on or in connection with which such use is likely to cause confusion, or to cause mistake, or to deceive shall be liable in a civil action by the registrant for the remedies provided in the Lanham act.[1] Thus, likelihood of confusion is primarily the legal basis for determining whether a party's use can be deemed an infringing use of a trademark, and, of course, such use must not be authorized by the registrant.

Additionally, the statutory definition applies to initial interest and post-sale confusion. *I.e.*, merely citing interest from others to look at and consider the goods or services is enough to establish confusion.

Since there is no statutory definition of what constitutes likelihood of confusion, the interpretation of likelihood of confusion has been left to the courts. Since the Supreme Court has not expressly defined how the term should be interpreted, the appellate courts have established the precedential basis for the standard of interpretation of "likelihood of confusion" in their respective districts. While many of the criteria used among the appellate courts to assess whether there is a likelihood of confusion are common, it is best to look at what has been expressly defined in the district where you are located.

For example, the Fourth Circuit Court of Appeals is the district where I commonly practice and includes the District of Maryland, the Eastern District of North Carolina, the Middle District of North Carolina, the Western District of North Carolina, the District of South Carolina, the Eastern District of Virginia, the Western District of Virginia, the Northern District of West Virginia and the Southern District of West Virginia.

---

[11] 15 U.S.C. § 1114.

In *Pizzeria Uno*, the Fourth Circuit Court of Appeals identified the following seven factors to use in determining whether there is a likelihood of confusion:[2]

1) the strength or distinctiveness of the mark;
2) the similarity of the two marks;
3) the similarity of the goods/services the marks identify;
4) the similarity of the facilities the two parties use in their businesses;
5) the similarity of the advertising used by the two parties;
6) the defendant's intent; and
7) actual confusion.

In a later case, the Fourth Circuit Court of Appeals included the following two additional factors that could be considered in the likelihood of confusion determination:[3]

8) the quality of the defendant's product; and
9) the sophistication of the consuming public.

However, the additional factors identified in *Sara Lee* are found to be applied less frequently than the *Pizzeria Uno* factors in determining whether there is a likelihood of confusion or not.

While a court need not find that each of the factors support likelihood of confusion or not, a court determines, based upon an analysis of applicable factors, whether, on balance, there is likelihood of confusion or not.

Strength or Distinctiveness of the Mark

Strength or distinctiveness of the mark is a paramount factor under the Fourth Circuit test.[4] Chapter 4 addresses where marks are within the distinctiveness spectrum. This factor identifies the ability of the mark to identify the goods or services with which the mark is associated.

---

[2] *Pizzeria Uno Corp. v. Temple*, 747 F.2d 1522, 224 USPQ 185 (4th Cir., 1984).
[3] *Sara Lee Corp. v. Kayser-Roth Corp.*, 81 F.3d 455, 463-64 (4th Cir., 1996).
[4] *Pizzeria Uno*, 747 F.2d at 1527.

As was noted in Chapter 4, descriptive marks are expressive types of marks that generally convey an immediate idea concerning the ingredients, qualities or characteristics of the goods or services. Descriptive marks must acquire distinctiveness or secondary meaning before they are capable of becoming subject to registration and becoming protectable based upon an examination conducted by the examining attorney in the USPTO.

Certain marks, such as descriptive marks, primarily geographically descriptive marks, marks that are primarily merely a surname and color marks, for example, are only registrable on the Principal Register with sufficient proof of acquired distinctiveness. It is incumbent on the party who is asserting distinctiveness to prove that such distinctiveness has been acquired by the mark.[5] The burden of proving that certain marks such as a color mark has acquired distinctiveness is substantial.[6]

Inherently distinctive marks such as arbitrary marks, fanciful marks and suggestive marks are considered strong marks. Trademarks that are characterized as inherently distinctive marks favor the registrant in a likelihood of confusion showing.

While a likelihood of confusion showing may be made in the case of non-inherently distinctive marks such as merely descriptive marks, personal name marks and primarily geographic descriptive marks, other factors in the likelihood of confusion test must be relied upon by the registrant. There is a presumption of validity when the USPTO determines the mark has acquire distinctiveness or has secondary meaning. Furthermore, marks that are registered in the USPTO without the need to prove secondary meaning are presumptively considered suggestive, but such a presumption may be rebutted by the defendant in court.

Secondary meaning is when "in the minds of the public, the primary significance of a [mark] is to identify the source of the

---

[5] 15 U.S.C. § 1052(f); *see Qualitex Co. v. Jacobson Prods. Co.*, 514 U.S. 159 (1995); *In re Owens-Corning Fiberglass Corp.*, 774 F.2d 1116, 1120-21 (Fed. Cir. 1985); *cf. Wal-Mart Stores, Inc. v. Samara Bros., Inc.*, 529 U.S. 205, 211-12 (2000).

[6] *See In re Owens-Corning Fiberglass*, 774 F.2d at 1131; TMEP §1212.05(a).

product rather than the product itself."[7] The extent of secondary meaning developed will be important in determining the strength or distinctiveness of the mark.

A mark that the registrant allows to commonly be used by third parties without challenging that use receives less protection than marks that are not in common use among parties. Such use even outside of registrant's field of use may also weaken the mark depending upon the extent of such use. However, other courts completely disregard this as evidence Marks that are determined to be generic or those that have become generic are not subject to trademark protection. Thus, likelihood of confusion cannot be found in these cases where the marks are not subject to or maintaining registration.

Similarity of the Two Marks

The test of similarity of the two marks establishes whether there exists a "similarity in appearance and sound which would result in confusion."[8] Additionally, similarity in meaning of the marks provide a reliable showing of similarity. Marks should be compared as they would be to the relevant consumer purchaser of the products or services associated with the marks. Goods and services are sufficiently related in a likelihood of confusions analysis if the average purchaser believes the goods or services came from the same source.

While courts may find that a mark has acquired distinctiveness allowing the mark to be registered, assuming such a mark avoids other bases for rejection such as, for example, ornamental nature of the mark, functional nature of the mark, and marks that have been genericized, courts require that the marks be compared with this similarity factor to consider in a likelihood of confusion analysis.

Similarity of the marks first may be driven by whether they are the same type of mark as discussed in Chapter 2. If the marks

---

[7] *Inwood Laboratories, Inc. v. Ives Laboratories, Inc.*, 456 U.S. 844, 851 (1982).

[8] *Petro Stopping Centers, L.P. v. James River Petroleum, Inc.*, 130 F.3d 88, 94 (4th Cir.1997) (*quoting Pizzeria Uno Corp.*, 747 F.2d at 1534).

have at least one type of attribute that is closely the same, then similarity of the marks may be established. For example, marks that are categorically the same type, such as word or words that are similar in nature, designs that have similar aspects, symbols that are similarly structured, a relatively common graphic shared by the marks, same or similar use of figures or numbers, or a common highlighted letter between the marks, may support a strong showing of similarity between the marks.

Generally, in the analysis, the marks may not be dissected. *I.e.*, the marks must be considered as a whole. But, in certain cases, similarity may be established when an essential part of the trademark that tends to have more weight in defining the mark when taken as a whole is shared by each of the marks. Clearly, marks may have generic features and focus may be placed on the essential non-generic portion. This may include similar design structures or common words, letters or figures that are somewhat essential to a message being delivered by the mark. While the allegedly infringing mark may still have other features, a similarity of an essential feature could support a finding of similarity of the marks.

Chapter 8 focuses upon the use of surveys. Survey evidence may assist in determining whether the marks substantially share similarity. However, as expressed in Chapter 8, such a comparison in surveys must be done in such a way that consumers normally view the products. Side-by-side comparisons may be done when the products at issue are typically found together on store shelves. In certain instances, consumers do not view the products in a side-by-side comparison. For example, products that may be more typically purchased over the Internet are usually not presented to the consumer in a side-by-side comparison. Also, capital intensive products or services are typically not presented in a side-by-side format. Therefore, the test must be formatted so that the consumer's state-of-mind when presented with the products as they normally would see them can be measured. Thus, the type of survey format used must be consistent with the way that consumers normally view the products or services.

Also, certain types of marks do not necessarily lend themselves to similarity of appearance. For example, likelihood of confusion for marks based on sound and scent would require a similarity analysis that goes beyond a visible sensation of the marks.

Similarity of the Goods/Services the Marks Identify

The comparison for the similarity or relatedness of the goods and/or services that the two marks are associated with is driven by a variety of factors. Factors weighing on this determination include whether the goods are part of the same broad category of goods, the relative sales price of the goods, and the competitiveness of the goods.[9]

Clearly, when the marks are associated with goods or services that belong in the same International Class of goods, then a similarity of goods can typically become more easily found. However, the description of the goods or services, and the uniqueness of features in those goods would also have some bearing on whether there is a similarity of goods or services shared between the marks. Additionally, the design and functionality of the goods will be determinative of whether the goods would be competitive or not.[10]

Similarity of the Facilities the Two Parties Use in Their Businesses

Similarities between the type of facility used by the parties to distribute products to the consuming public is relevant to the issue of likelihood of confusion.[11] Typically, the types of facilities used for the sale of the goods or services are ordinarily subject to this test, because this becomes the venue the buyer experiences in the purchase of the goods or services. Thus, this analysis first requires identifying who the consuming public is and where they

---

[9] *Maker's Mark Distillery, Inc. v. Diageo N. Am., Inc.*, 679 F.3d 410, 423 (6th Cir., 2012).

[10] *Traffix Devices Inc. v. Marketing Displays Inc.*, 532 U.S. 23 (2001).

[11] *Pizzeria Uno Corp. v. Temple*, 566 F. Supp. 385 (D. S.C., 1983) (*quoting Amstar Corp. v. Domino's Pizza, Inc.*, 615 F.2d 252, 262 (5th Cir.1980)).

typically shop or seek out the particular types of products or services at issue.

If the goods are ordinary consumer goods generally purchase by the public, then such goods will commonly be found in a store aisle or online, and the similarity of facilities substantially become the same. However, more specialty products that require a different sales venue may have facilities that are not at all similar in nature. For example, maybe the venue is to fit the product to the consumer, and the facilities required for this could be of a different design.

Similarity of overall marketplace use in the facilities where the products or services are found may also have significance. For example, packaging, presentation and display appearance of the associated products may show a likelihood of confusion.

Facilities need not only be those associated with those that sale the goods. Manufacturing venues may be at issue for certain industrial products particularly when the purchasing consumers go there to decide on whether they should purchase a product or not or to inspect or check out products that have been manufactured for them. A manufacturing factory that supports the subassembly of products to keep in inventory and distribute such products differs from, for example, fabrication shops for the manufacture of specialty types of equipment, and can support a finding against similarity of facilities if this is the primary point of sale for those that purchase these types of products.

Similarity of the Advertising Used by the Two Parties

Advertising by the registrant tends to build the strength of the mark and the recognition of the brand with which the mark is associated. If third parties advertise the allegedly infringing mark in much the same way as the registrant, then this could dilute the strength of the mark otherwise established by the registrant.

Channels of sale and advertising of the products or services has an impact on whether these factors are applicable or not.[12] If it is conducive to sale or market the respective products or services using the same or similar means of advertising, then it further shows the products or services have some similarity, and marketing or selling the products via the same avenue presents a potential for likelihood of confusion.

However, the failure of a party to place a significant emphasis on advertising a distinguishing feature of the mark or even perhaps the mark itself makes the similarity in advertising used by the two parties less significant.[13]

Defendant's Intent

Defendant's intent is a triable question of fact. If it can be shown that defendant had actual knowledge of the registered trademark, but yet actively chose to use the mark in a manner similar to that by the registrant, then some support for likelihood of confusion may further be found. Bad faith may be established by:

- Defendant's copying of type style, background designs, color schemes or overall trade dress.[14]
- Defendant's absence of credible, good faith explanation for adoption of the mark.[15]
- Defendant's admission of use of the mark to influence consumers.[16]

The Federal Circuit has implied that this factor has less of a bearing on a finding of likelihood of confusion. Even if intent

---

[12] *See, e.g., Louis Vuitton Malletier v. Haute Diggity Dog*, 507 F.3d 252, 262-63 (4th Cir., 2007).

[13] *Cf. Shakespeare Co. v. Silstar Corp. of America, Inc.*, 906 F.Supp. 997, 1012 (D. S.C., 1996).

[14] *Spring Mills, Inc. v. Ultracashmere House, Ltd.*, 689 F.2d 1127, 1134-35 (2d Cir., 1982).

[15] *Playboy Enterprises, Inc. v. Chuckleberry Pub., Inc.*, 687 F.2d 563 (2nd Cir., 1982).

[16] *Board of Supervisors for La State v. Smack Apparel*, 550 F.3d 465 (5th Cir., 2008).

can be demonstrated, "[a] defendant's conduct, whether legitimate or reprehensible, has only a tenuous connection to the perceptions of consumers …"[17]

As noted above, defendant must have some form of notice of the registration of the trademark. The failure of the plaintiff to provide notice of the registration is a mitigating factor.[18]

Opinions of counsel may at times be used as a defense as well. However, mere reliance on the opinion of counsel may or may not absolve the defendant of a finding of bad faith. For example, it has been argued that a defendant's belief they needed to seek legal counsel demonstrated that they had the intent to trade upon the goodwill of the mark. However, if the defendant's general course of procedure is to obtain an opinion of counsel in all such instances of adoption of a mark, then this should be sufficient to overcome such a argument.

Actual Confusion

Actual confusion is deemed one of the most important of the seven factor *Pizzeria Uno* likelihood of confusion test.[19] However, evidence of actual confusion may be difficult find.

Actual confusion can be demonstrated by primarily anecdotal evidence.[20] Some have even argued that isolated instances of actual confusion cannot be persuasive. Additionally, evidence of only a small number of instances of actual confusion may be dismissed as de minimis.[21]

---

[17] *Decorations for Generations, Inc. v. Home Depot USA, Inc.*, No. 04-1072 (Fed. Cir. 3/8/2005) (Fed. Cir., 2005) (*quoting Continental Lab. Prods., Inc. v. Medax Int'l, Inc.*, 114 F. Supp. 2d 992, 1012-13 (S.D. Cal. 2000)).

[18] *Holiday Inns, Inc. v. Holiday Inn*, 645 F.2d 239, 248 (4th Cir., 1981) (*quoting* 15 U.S.C. § 1111) ("… in any suit for infringement under this chapter by such a registrant failing to give such notice of registration, no profits and no damages shall be recovered under the provisions of this chapter unless the defendant had actual notice of the registration").

[19] *George & Co. LLC v. Imagination Entertainment Ltd.*, 575 F.3d 383, 398 (4th Cir., 2009).

[20] *Tools USA and Equip. Co. v. Champ Frame Straightening Equip., Inc.*, 87 F.3d 654, 661 (4th Cir.1996).

[21] *Petro Stopping Ctrs., L.P. v. James River Petroleum, Inc.*, 130 F.3d 88, 95 (4th Cir. 1997); see also McCarthy § 23:14.

Quality of the Defendant's Product

Consideration of the quality of the defendant's product is most appropriate in situations involving the production of cheap copies or knockoffs of a competitor's trademark-protected goods.[22] A defendant's product that is markedly inferior is likely to be highly probative of its reliance on the similarity of the two marks to generate undeserved sales. *Id.*

Sophistication of the Consuming Public

A market having extremely sophisticated buyers does not allow a likelihood of consumer confusion to be presumed on the basis of the similarity in trade name alone.[23] The typical buyer is more discerning and less easily confused when purchasing expensive items.[24]

Clearly, sophisticated consumers may be expected to exercise a greater degree of care. The following levels of consumer purchasers have been identified:

- Public Versus Professional – The public is considered those purchases that are driven by appearance and general impressions. The professional typically is buying for a specific purpose and imposes greater knowledge and discrimination in a purchase decision.
- Ordinarily Prudent Purchaser – Notwithstanding the type of purchaser, the purchaser is considered to exercise the care normally exercised by the "ordinarily prudent" purchaser of the goods in issue. Ordinary prudence varies with the type of product being purchased. The expense of the product, the method of sales and the channels of distribution may influence the degree of ordinary prudence. For example, a buyer generally exercises greater care in their purchase of more expensive goods, but even

---

22 *Sara Lee*, 81 F.3d at 467.
23 *Perini Corp. v. Perini Constr., Inc.*, 915 F.2d 121, 128 (4th Cir., 1990).
24 *Fortune Dynamic, Inc. v. Victoria's Secret Stores Brand Mgmt. Inc.*, 618 F.3d 1025, 1038 (9th Cir., 2010).

relatively inexpensive goods are purchased by sophisticated and knowledgeable persons.

- Impulse Purchases – Impulse purchases, regardless of where purchased, are typically not subject to a high degree of examination prior to purchase. The impulsive nature of purchases has been a factor in supporting a finding of likelihood of confusion in certain cases.[25]
- Capital Intensive Purchases – Capital intensive purchases involve more sophisticated discerning buyers. Sophisticated purchasers are expected to be less easily confused and favors the alleged infringer. However, lower priced consumer products or services likely involve either less sophisticated purchasers or a reduced level of review of the purchase. Thus, these types of products are more likely to incite a likelihood of confusion.

---

[25] *See, e.g., Beer Nuts, Inc. v. Clover Club Foods Co.*, 711 F.2d 934, 941 (10th Cir., 1983).

CHAPTER 8: Survey Evidence

Survey evidence has become a more frequently used, but expensive type of evidence used in determining likelihood of confusion as well as other mitigating factors such as whether a mark bears secondary meaning and other analyses as further discussed in this Chapter. This Chapter also provides an overview of the survey process to provide more insight for brand developers in the process of how the relevant universe of users are identified, and how a sample of that universe is surveyed in an attempt to evaluate relevant factors included for analysis in the survey. Clearly, the universe encompasses the people that the brand is attempting to market to and become the buyers of the process.

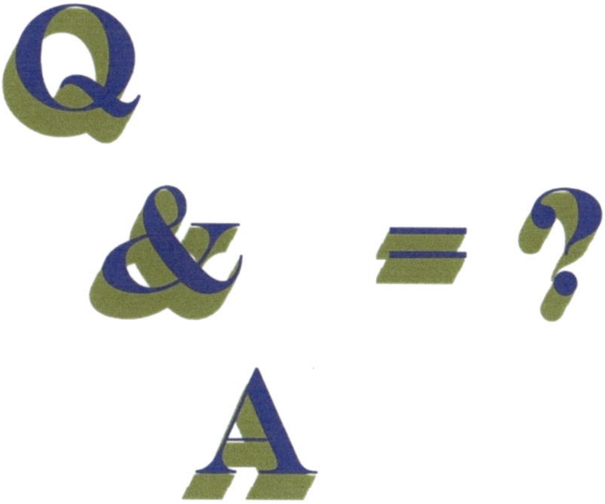

At times, this Chapter refers to "senior mark" and "junior mark." For purposes of our discussions, the "senior mark" is the mark that has been registered in the USPTO as a trademark, and the "junior mark" is the mark that is considered the allegedly infringing mark.

Expert witnesses specializing in conducting surveys, developing expert reports, being subjected to depositions, preparation for and actual testimony at trial typically have rather high hourly billing rates. Just the mere development of the survey can have an expense running upwards from $50,000 to $100,000. Once it is all said and done, if the case does go to trial, the survey and associated expert fees could be $200,000 or more.

In many instances, motions in limine are filed to exclude the expert testimony of the survey expert in an effort to prevent the results of the survey from being introduced at trial. In some cases, these motions are granted causing those fees associated with development of the survey results from being altogether lost. Therefore, it is very critical that the guidance that has been somewhat well-established in the development and use of surveys is diligently followed.

Generally, the following factors are considered important when conducting a survey:

1). The proper universe was selected and examined;
2). A representative sample was drawn from that universe;
3). The mode of questioning the interviewees was correct;
4). The persons conducting the survey are recognized experts;
5). The data gathered were accurately reported;
6). The sample design, the questionnaire and the interviewing were in accordance with generally accepted standards of objective procedure and statistics in the field of such surveys;
7). The sample design and the interviews were conducted independently of the attorneys; and
8). The interviewers trained in this field had no knowledge of the litigation or the purposes for which the survey was used.

Sampling Universe

Typically, the first step in designing a survey is to determine the "universe" to be studied. The universe is that segment of the population whose perceptions and states of mind are relevant to the issues in the case. The universe may be narrowed from the population at large in various ways: geographically (people living in the geographic region); commercially (retail dealers or consumers);

according to buying habits (prospective purchasers of the type of product or service at issue); or by any other meaningful criteria that the law sets down as limiting or defining the class of persons whose state of mind is at issue. A survey of the wrong universe offers no probative value to the litigation.

Once the universe is identified, a "sample" to be surveyed is identified from that universe. Typically, taking a census of the entire universe would be difficult and prohibitive. Instead, the sample is a subset of the universe that is capable through mathematical and statistical probability models that is reasonably projected to be representative of the universe.

The methods used in conducting the survey must conform to generally recognized statistical standards. Relevant factors include the following:

- The population was properly chosen and defined;
- The sample chosen was representative of that population;
- The data gathered were accurately reported; and
- The data were analyzed in accordance with accepted statistical principles.

Examples of proper universes that have been accepted by courts include the following:

- *Light Bulbs and Flashlights.* To prove secondary meaning and likelihood of confusion among purchasers of bulbs, lamps, batteries and flashlights, the relevant universe is the general population since everyone buys such goods.
- *Restaurant Services.* To prove that people would be confused as to an association between defendant's BEEFEATER restaurant and plaintiff's BEEFEATER gin, a survey conducted among 500 male and female heads-of-household within a five-mile radius of defendant's proposed restaurant was found to be a relevant universe.
- *Children's Products.* Secondary meaning and confusion surveys of children ages 8-18 were held to be proper as to

the significance of a trademark in the pattern of soles on children's sneakers.

- *International Adventure Services.* Proper universe for likelihood of dilution for the use of G.A.P Adventures in association with such services dilutes GAP mark related to clothing are men and women 18 years of age or older who were likely, within the next year, to use the Internet to search for information on travel tours outside the continental United States.
- *Detection of Disease using Laboratory Tests.* The proper universe for a confusion survey of blood test products was composed of those consumers age 21 and older who would consider using blood-testing services to analyze nutritional needs.

Over-Inclusive Universes

Over-inclusive universes attempt to encompass such a large number of persons allowing them to include those whose perceptions are irrelevant. An over-inclusive universe tends to improperly skew the results of the survey with the inclusion of the irrelevant information.

Examples of over-inclusive universes include the following:

- *Weight Loss.* Over-inclusive universe comprising women between the ages of 18 and 55 who (1) had purchased frozen food entrees in the past six months and (2) had tried to lose weight through diet or exercise in the past year in association with the use of LEAN CUISINE mark on frozen diet entrees.
- *Sneakers.* Over-inclusive universe of prospective and prior purchasers of "sneakers" ranging in price from $10 to $200 in attempting to establish actual confusion.
- *Moderately Priced Wines.* Survey of adults who had or were likely to buy a bottle of wine in the $5 to $14 price range

was too broad of price range when testing reaction to moderately priced wines.

Under-Inclusive Universes

Under-inclusive universes define a group that is narrower than the ideal universe resulting in leaving out a group of persons whose perception is relevant.

Examples of under-inclusive universes include the following:

- *Basketballs.* Failure to include persons in the market to buy a basketball is under-inclusive in a survey to establish whether a red, white and blue basketball had acquired secondary meaning.
- *Beanbag Animals.* Limiting the universe to girls from the ages of 13 to 18 years old was under-inclusive in a survey to establish genericness of the use of BEANIES for beanbag animals.
- *Ceramic Decorative Tiles.* Universe found to be under-inclusive by only including interior designers in a case involving a survey trade dress infringement of ceramic decorative tiles when it failed to also include builders, architects, contractors, and homeowners.
- *Cosmetic Product.* A universe skewed towards a younger population was under-inclusive when almost three-quarters of the market for the cosmetic product included persons over 34 years of age.

Forward versus Reverse Confusion

In a case that claims forward confusion, the proper universe to survey is composed of buyers of the goods or services having the allegedly infringing mark and not the plaintiff's user's customers, which are included in a reverse confusion survey. Using the senior user's customers in the universe is considered too be under-inclusive through narrowing the universe. On the other hand, surveying only potential customers of the defendant's product having the allegedly infringing mark and omitting potential customers of the plaintiff's product, may skew the results of a confusion survey upward so as to substantially detract from the weight of the survey.

Approximating Market Conditions

The survey method should as closely as possible replicate the situation in which the ordinary person would encounter the goods or services having the trademark. Survey interviews may be conducted in a store or a shopping mall, over the Internet or by telephone.

Probability versus Non-Probability Surveys

A probability survey involves the mathematically random selection of persons from the defined universe. A probability sample permits a statistical projection of the results to the universe as a whole, with a known degree of error. Typically, probability surveys are conducted via a telephone survey by randomly selecting telephone numbers in a certain geographic region. However, telephone surveys have a disadvantage in that a greater number of people through caller ID and call blocking.

Probability surveys, however, are costly and difficult to implement. Furthermore, randomness can only be maintained when each household member has a random chance of picking up the call.

Non-probability sampling, sometimes call mail-intercept surveys, does not have a randomness requirement. The selection of respondents to question is usually done on the basis of availability at a designated location—typically a shopping mall. Non-probability surveys are the most popular type of in-person survey conducted.

Indeed, Jacob Jacoby, an expert who had years of experience conducting research on survey methods, concluded that probability sampling for trademark surveys is, generally speaking, an unrealizable ideal, and insisted that probability sampling for trademark surveys makes little practical sense.[1]

<u>Internet Surveys</u>

A survey conducted via the Internet is appropriate since Internet purchasers commonly encounter trademarks and make purchasing decisions on that platform. Especially given the increasing difficulty of reaching people who are willing to be interviewed by phone and the reluctance of people to be interviewed in person at a shopping mall, surveys conducted over the Internet have become more common in trademark and false advertising cases. Courts are convinced that these types of surveys are necessary.

In order to be admissible and reliable, an Internet survey must attempt to replicate as nearly as possible the actual conditions under which Internet users are likely to encounter products or services bearing the trademarks. Internet surveys have the advantage of screening large populations quickly allowing contact with small groups of people that are still representative of the identified universe.

Survey Formats

There are two survey formats that have commonly been used to test for confusion—the "Eveready" format and the "Squirt" format. The Eveready format is appropriate when the senior mark is strong and widely recognized. Since the senior mark is so well-known, the Eveready form does expressly show respondents the senior mark.

The Squirt format works under the assumption that the senior mark is not well known and presents the respondent with both the senior mark and the junior mark. There are both a "direct" method and a "subtle" method for presenting the

---

[1] Jacoby, Trademark Surveys, § 6.70 (ABA 2014) ("[I]n those relatively few instances where probability and nonprobability surveys have been directed toward examining the same issue in the same universe, the theorized superiority of probability surveys has not always materialized." Jacoby, Trademark Surveys, at § 6.35.).

respondent with the senior mark. The direct method asks in some fashion if the respondent thinks that goods or services bearing the senior mark and junior mark, interchangeably presented however, are from the same source or different sources.

The more subtle form of the Squirt survey is to include a product-lineup survey where the respondent is shown an array of branded products and asked questions about the relation between the companies that sell the products with the contesting marks. Courts will only admit this survey format if it includes a significant number of real-world products in which both marks will be seen in the marketplace in a side-by-side format. Indeed, it is deemed that presenting products in a side-by-side format in the survey when they are not normally seen like that in the marketplace will skew the results of the survey.

Improper Methods for Surveys

The majority rule among courts is that while technical deficiencies can reduce a survey's weight, they will not prevent the survey from being admitted into evidence. In essence, if a survey is able to pass the criteria that it has proper foundation, it can be admitted into evidence, and it is up to the trier of fact to assess the nature and quality of the survey evidence in order to decide how much weight that the survey results deserves.

<u>Examples of Methodological Deficiencies</u>

Location. Questioning an interviewee in a location where they could see or had just seen the goods and labels in question.

Irrelevant Questions. Examples include:

- Asking ambiguous question or one that is not relevant to the issue.
- Asking for a ranking of "similarities" between the junior and senior marks.
- Showing photographs that have been "doctored" or not representative of the product sold.
- Asking questions about the logo without showing the logo as it actually appeared on the product.

- Asking questions about an unpackaged product, which otherwise always appears in its marked packaging.
- Showing products side-by-side bearing the senior user's and junior user's marks when that is not the way they normally appear in the marketplace.
- Survey is designed to show point-of-sale confusion, but plaintiff's theory is post-sale confusion.

Tabulation Problems. Treating inconclusive responses as unqualified responses, changing survey to record certain responses and changing recorded responses.

Bias Problems. Use of inducements to encourage participation in survey.

Timing Problems. Taking a survey some years beyond when a showing of secondary meaning was attempting to be made.

Insufficient Number of Responses. The number of respondents must be mathematically significant to extrapolate to the targeted group in the universe.

Allowing Viewing of Stimulus While Qestioning. J. B. Schwann, a notable expert on survey design, determined that keeping the stimulus in view while questioning ("reading test") is only appropriate for assessing point-of-sale confusion.[2] H. D. Ostberg, another noted expert in survey design, determined that removing the stimulus during questioning ("memory test") is typically more representative of the buying process.[3] Ostberg concluded that consumers in the real world obtain information on their own prior to purchase without being led by an interviewer's questions, and this is replicated when the interviewer instructs the respondent to look at the products as they would normally when expecting to conduct a purchase.

---

2 J.B. Swann, A "Reading" Test or a "Memory" Test: Which Survey Methodology is Correct?, 95 Trademark Rptr. 876 (2005).

3 H.D. Ostberg, Response to the Article Entitled A "Reading" Test or a "Memory" Test: Which Survey Methodology is Correct?, 95 Trademark Rptr. 1446 (2005)

Avoidance of Leading Questions

Questions must be avoided that attempt to lead the respondent to a desired conclusion.

Minimize Demand Effects. "Demand Effects" are produced in a survey when respondents use cues from the questions or procedural format to infer the purpose of the survey in an attempt to identify what they believe are the answers being sought.

Slanted Questions. Posing questions in such a format that lead an interviewee to a desired response in a critical question.

Implying Connection between the Parties. It is improper to ask interviewee if the marks are from the same or different sources. Courts have construed these types of questions as improperly leading since it appears to suggest a connection that may have not occurred to the respondent.

It has been found that it is not leading to present the possibility to respondents that there may be some form of affiliation or licensing behind a junior user's operation and use of the associated mark.

Control Cell

A properly conducted survey should include a control cell. In the control cell, the respondents do not receive the same stimulant as the test group receives. This will allow comparison results between responses of the test group and the responses of the control group to relatively compare the extent of deviations that should exist between the responses from these groups.

A control cell allows for the removal of "general background noise" that may exist in the survey figures. This noise could be the result of respondents answering with their preexisting views rather than focusing upon the survey stimulus. Also, some respondents may simply always be inclined to answer yes to any question, while other respondents quickly guess since they would prefer to simply get the survey out of the way. The control group likely has similar types of people participating allowing for their responses to be filtered from the survey results.

The net rate of confusion would be the raw confusion rate measured from the test cell reduced by the rate found in the control cell. For example, a test cell yielding a 25% "raw" rate of confusion but reduced by 20% as a result of noise results in only a 5% actual rate of confusion. Such a rate has been found not support a finding of likelihood of confusion from survey results.[4]

The general principle for choosing an appropriate control is for it to share as many characteristics with the experimental stimulus as possible, with the key exception of the characteristic whose influence is being assessed.[5] The control question or questions should use a mark similar enough to the actual mark that it provides an accurate measure of the confusion created by the accused mark, not by some other similarity.[6]

Laying a Foundation for Survey Evidence

The party offering a survey has the burden of laying a foundation that the survey was conducted in a manner that is consistent with accepted principles of survey research. The following is a recommended list of seven factors to consider in laying the foundation for a survey:

1) The population was properly chosen and defined;
2) The sample chosen was representative of that population;
3) The data gathered were accurately reported;
4) The data were analyzed in accordance with accepted statistical principles;
5) The questions asked were clear and not leading;

---

4 *Reed-Union Corp. v. Turtle Wax, Inc.*, 77 F.3d 909, 912 (7th Cir., 1996) ("To estimate the 'normal' rates of confusion, each expert used a different pair of products." Affirmed the lower court's reliance on the defendant's expert's choice of a control stimulus rather than on that used by the plaintiff's expert.).

5 S. S. Diamond, Control Foundations: Rationales and Approaches, in Trademark and Deceptive Advertising Surveys, 210 (ABA, Eds Diamond & Swann 2012).

6 *Valador, Inc. v. HTC Corp.*, 242 F.Supp.3d 448, 459-1 (E.D. Va., 2017).

6) The survey was conducted by qualified persons following proper interview procedures; and
7) The process was conducted so as to ensure objectivity (*e.g.*, was the survey conducted in anticipation of litigation and by persons connected with the parties or counsel or aware of its purpose in the litigation?).

Content of Survey Reports

The Federal Judicial Center Reference Manual on Scientific Evidence recommends that a survey report demonstrate the trustworthiness of the survey and the professionalism of the testifying survey expert. As such, the final survey report should describe the following items in detail:

1) The purpose of the survey;
2) A definition of the target population and a description of the sampling frame;
3) A description of the sample design, including the method of selecting respondents, the method of interview, the number of callbacks, respondent eligibility or screening criteria and method, and other pertinent information;
4) A description of the results of sample implementation, including the number of (a) potential respondents contacted, (b) potential respondents not reached, (c) noneligibles, (d) refusals, (e) incomplete interviews or terminations, and (f) completed interviews;
5) The exact wording of the questions used, including a copy of each version of the actual questionnaire, interviewer instructions, and visual exhibits;
6) A description of any special scoring (*e.g.*, grouping of verbatim responses into broader categories);
7) A description of any weighting or estimating procedures used;
8) Estimates of the sampling error, where appropriate (*i.e.*, in probability samples);

9) Statistical tables clearly labeled and identified regarding the source of the data, including the number of raw cases forming the base for each table, row, or column; and
10) Copies of interviewer instructions, validation results, and code books.

Survey Results

Actual Confusion

While survey evidence is sometimes connected to actual confusion, survey evidence is circumstantial evidence, not direct evidence, of likelihood of confusion; thus, survey evidence cannot be considered as measuring the degree of actual confusion. Instead, surveys are an experimental environment from which useful data concerning the likelihood that actual confusion will take place.

Likelihood of Confusion

Likelihood of confusion is the likelihood present among a "substantial" or "appreciable" number of reasonably prudent customers. Findings of confusion among 25% to 50% can be relied upon as a showing of likelihood of confusion. Courts have even accepted numbers lower than that—down to 15%—declaring the number as neither small nor de minimus. The number appears to have to slip below 10% in most cases before a court will determine that the survey results do not support a likelihood of confusion.

Including Those Who Do Not Know the Senior Mark

When testing confusion among respondents in a "forward" confusion case, the computation of the relevant "confused" percentage should also include those persons who were not aware of the senior user's mark. Excluding these persons would skew the percentage results upwards and fail to accurately represent the state of mind of all persons who are likely to see or buy the junior user's product.

Secondary Meaning

It has also been held that when surveying for secondary meaning of trade dress, it is improper to discard the views of those who were not familiar with the trade dress. Courts have tended to require a greater percentage of survey respondents to support a finding of secondary meaning. The survey results appear to mostly need to exceed 40% before a court will find that the survey results support a showing of secondary meaning.

Generic Name

The test at stake is determining whether the target group in the survey believes the mark to be a generic name or a trademark. Surveys in determining whether a mark is or has become generic have somewhat become *de facto* important among courts. Generally, courts accept that the majority view on the status of the mark is the determinative view in surveys for determining whether marks are generic.

Judicial Acceptance of Survey Evidence

Surveys have evolved to be more sophisticated and scientific in nature; thus, survey evidence is now more commonly used in trademark litigation. However, courts are not adverse to dismissing the use of survey data when the approach does not comply with a well-established methodology or the survey suffers from incriminating deficiencies. On the other hand, some courts have questioned why plaintiffs, in certain cases, have not introduced survey evidence. Courts do, however, extend the view that survey evidence is not necessary in every case.

CHAPTER 9: Damages & Monetary Relief

Monetary Relief for Trademark Infringement

The Lanham Act provides that a violation of a right of a registered mark entitles the plaintiff, *subject to the principles of equity*, the following:[1]

- Defendant's profits upon plaintiff proving defendant's sales with this amount reduced by costs or deductions as shown by defendant.
- Damages sustained by the plaintiff.
- Costs of the action, and, in exceptional cases, an award of reasonable attorneys' fees to the prevailing party.

In assessing defendant's profits, the plaintiff is required to only prove the defendant's sales. Defendant has the burden of proving all elements of cost reductions claimed.

If the court finds that the amount of the recovery based on profits is either inadequate or excessive, the court may, in its discretion, enter judgment for such sum as the court shall find to be just, according to the circumstances of the case. By statute, any sum that exceeds the amount determined to be actual damages may not be more than three times that amount. Any amount awarded by the court must be considered compensation and not a penalty.

<u>Plaintiff's Proof of Sales</u>

The plaintiff is required to prove the defendant's sales only, and the court considers defendant's sales to be profit unless the defendant can prove "all elements of cost or deduction claimed."[2] When exact ascertainment of the amount of damages is precluded, plaintiff may recover upon a showing of the extent of damages as

---

[1] 15 U.S.C. § 1117(a)

[2] *Muhler Co. v. Window World of N. Charleston LLC*, Case No. No. 2:11-cv-00851-DCN, pg. 12 of unpublished opinion (D. S.C., 2014).

a matter of just and reasonable inference, although the result may be only an approximation.[3]

Defendant's Costs or Deductions for Calculation of Profit

Calculation of Offsets. The burden of proving any deduction for sales not based on the infringing mark falls upon the infringer.[4] The court must analyze the claimed cost set-offs "with particular rigor," requiring the court to "give extra scrutiny to the categories of overhead expenses claimed by the infringer to insure that each category is directly and validly connected to the sale and production of the infringing product."[5]

Direct Cost of Goods Sold. The deduction may include manufacture, labor, packing and administrative costs associated with the infringing item.[6] The costs associated with third party advertising of the infringing goods may be a legitimate deduction.[7] Flaws in the deduction of costs render the costs unreliable and inadmissible.[8]

Increases in Overhead Expenses. With respect to costs or deductions to reduce the sales to find profits, a proportionate amount of overhead expenses may not be claimed when no overall increase in overhead expenses is found to be attributable to the sales of the infringing item.[9] The defendant must prove that sales of the infringing items actually contributed to the production and distribution or sales of the infringing goods in calculating the amount of overhead expenses to be deducted from the sales.[10]

---

[3] *Ramada Inns, Inc. v. Gadsden Motel Co.*, 804 F.2d 1562, 1565 (11th Cir. 1986)).

[4] *Int'l Star Class Yacht Racing Ass'n v. Tommy Hilfiger U.S.A.*, 146 F.3d 66, 72 (2d Cir., 1998)

[5] *Audemars Piguet Holding S.A. v. Swiss Watch Int'l., Inc.*, 42 F.Supp.3d 540, 544 (S.D.N.Y. 2014).

[6] *Dolori Fabrics, Inc. v. Limited, Inc.*, 662 F.Supp. 1347, 1356 (S.D. N.Y., 1987).

[7] *Playboy Enterprises, Inc. v. Dumas*, 831 F.Supp. 295, 319 (S.D. N.Y., 1993).

[8] *Teaching Co. Ltd. Partner. v. Unapix Entertainment*, 87 F.Supp.2d 567, 591 (E.D. Va., 2000).

[9] *Maltina Corp. v. Cawy Bottling Co., Inc.*, 613 F.2d 582, 586-87 (5th Cir., 1980).

[10] *Kamar Intern., Inc. v. Russ Berrie and Co., Inc.*, 752 F.2d 1326, 1333 (9th Cir., 1984).

Costs of the Action

A finding of trademark infringement entitles plaintiff to court costs for this action, as expressly granted by statute. The term "costs of this action" must be interpreted with reference to "costs" defined in 28 U.S.C. § 1920, which include fees and disbursements for the clerk, marshal, court reporter, experts, witnesses, interpreters, printing, copies and transcript.[11]

Attorneys' Fees

The court may award reasonable attorney fees, but only in "exceptional cases."[12] The Fourth Circuit defines an exceptional case as one in which the party's conduct was "malicious, fraudulent, willful or deliberate in nature."[13]

The United States Supreme Court has directed that the term "exceptional case" should be as found in 35 U.S.C. § 285 in the Patent Act.[14] The Fourth Circuit has chosen to apply the *Octane Fitness* interpretation to an exceptional case under 15 U.S.C. § 1117(a) in the Lanham Act.[15] The determination is made in light of the totality of the circumstances:

1) there is an unusual discrepancy in the merits of the positions taken by the parties, based on the non-prevailing party's position as either frivolous or objectively unreasonable;
2) the non-prevailing party has litigated the case in an unreasonable manner; or
3) there is otherwise the need in particular circumstances to advance considerations of compensation and deterrence.

---

[11] *Radiance Found., Inc. v. Nat'l Ass'n for the Advancement of Colored People*, Civil Action No 2:13cv53, unpublished opinion pp. 47-8 (E.D. Va., 2014).

[12] 15 U.S.C. § 1117(a).

[13] *People for Ethical Treatment of Animals v. Doughney*, 263 F. 3d 359, 370 (4th Cir. 2001); *Tools USA & Equip. Co. v. Champ Frame Straightening Equip., Inc.*, 885 F. Supp. 141, 144 (M.D.N.C.1994), aff'd, 87 F.3d 654 (4th Cir. 1996).

[14] *Octane Fitness, LLC v. Icon Health*, 134 S.Ct. 1749 (2014).

[15] *Verisign, Inc. v. Xyz.Com LLC*, 891 F.3d 481, 482-83 (4th Cir., 2018).

Factors Courts Use in Determining Damages

In addition to the statutory formula for actual damages, courts have latitude to impose an additional amount as long as that amount does not exceed three times the amount determined to be actual damages. Factors that are influential on the court in determining a damage award include the following:

- defendant's willful infringement or bad faith;
- plaintiff's lost sales due to infringement;
- extent of other remedies to redress injury (*e.g.*, injunctive relief);
- any unreasonable delay by plaintiff in asserting rights;
- public interest in making infringing misconduct unprofitable; and
- defendant's "palming off" its products as plaintiffs.

Principles of Equity

The principles of equity standard is established based upon such terms as the court deems reasonable as has been well-established by equity courts in many types of equity cases over the course of precedential history. Courts may find that, under the principles of equity, injunctive relief may sufficiently compensate the registrant for any infringing activity. By statute, courts are granted authority for injunctive relief under the Lanham Act.[16] The following must be demonstrated:

1) plaintiff has suffered an irreparable injury;
2) remedies available at law are inadequate to compensate for the injury;
3) considering the balance of hardships between the plaintiff and defendant, a remedy in equity is warranted; and

---

[16] 15 U.S. Code § 1116.

4) the public interest would not be disserved by a permanent injunction.

Equitable defenses also may impact any monetary relief or damages. For example, a court may determine that laches or registrant's delay in asserting its rights impacts the extent of any damage award. Additionally, it is within the court's discretion to fashion an award of profits that it finds equitable, based upon its own calculations.[17]

Counterfeit Marks

A counterfeit mark is defined as a counterfeit of a mark that is registered on the principal register for such goods or services sold, or a spurious designation is identical with, or substantially indistinguishable from, a designation of the mark as disclosed in the Act. In a case involving a counterfeit mark or designation, except on a finding of extenuating circumstances, the court shall enter a judgment of three times profits or damages, whichever amount is greater. The violation must include:

- Intentional use of a mark or designation knowing such mark is a counterfeit mark; or
- Providing goods or services necessary to the commission of a violation of the above.

Prior to judgment being rendered in a case involving a counterfeit mark, the plaintiff may instead elect statutory damages instead of the treble damages identified above. An award of statutory damages for any such use in connection with the sale, offering for sale, or distribution of goods or services in the amount of:

1) Not less than $1,000 or more than $200,000 per counterfeit mark per type of goods or services sold, offered for sale, or distributed, as the court considers just; or

---

[17] *Synergistic Intern., LLC v. Korman*, 402 F.Supp.2d 651, 666 (E.D. Va., 2005).

2) If the court finds that the use of the counterfeit mark was willful, not more than $2,000,000 per counterfeit mark per type of goods or services sold, offered for sale or distributed, as the court considers just.

A determination that the violation is willful is a rebuttable presumption.

State Law Claims Associated with Trademark Infringement

In addition to any Federal claims asserted for trademark infringement, there are typically state claims that may be made in an effort to capture damages as well. For cases brought in a Federal District Court, the Court has jurisdiction based upon federal question and supplemental jurisdiction may be invoked for claims made under statutory or common law of the state where the action is based.

State law claims may include common law trademark infringement for rights established based upon first to use or statutory infringement for marks that have been registered in the state. Additionally, there may be other statutory grounds for the defendant's unauthorized use of the mark in connection with goods or services. For example, North Carolina has statutes for unfair and deceptive trade practices (N.C.G.S. § 75-1.1) that may apply. Similarly, South Carolina has an Unfair Trade Practices Act (South Carolina Code Ann. § 39-5-10 *et seq*) that could be applicable in that state. The laws of the state where the case is being tried must be reviewed in order to determine additional state claims that may be asserted.

Finally, the common law unjust enrichment may be asserted as well, which relies upon the black letter law established by court precedent in the determination of whether it applies or not.

CHAPTER 10: Alternatives to Litigation

Settlement

Many times, litigation is like a roll of the dice or a spin of

the roulette wheel. While you may believe that you have an open-and-shut case, you will likely find over the course of discovery, that there are more issues involved that can complicate the process and add to uncertainty whether you will be successful or not. Many practitioners attempt to identify the probability of success and the total damages that may be awarded. Multiplying the probability of success and this total damage estimate gives what is known as the risk-adjusted return. Mathematically speaking, while this may not be your return, the percentage of people operating under the same probability of success to receive the same estimated damage award will be successful, while 100 less the percentage of people operating under the same probability of success will not recover. So, on average, all parties—the winners and the losers—will on average capture the risk adjusted return with some capturing nothing and others capturing the full amount or somewhere in between.

Its always good to maintain a sense of the status of your probability of success and the amount of potential damages at stake. This will give you some sense of where you may want to consider settling over the course of mediation and other similar discussions that may arise over the course of the litigation. Consequently, the opposing party or parties will be operating under a similar risk-adjusted potential for loss. So, in an ideal world, the parties would agree to settle for the risk-adjusted amount since this will allow much of the additional costs of litigation to be forgone, and the payout would be equivalent to the risk adjusted exposure.

As the litigation continues, the probability of success will be subject to adjustment based upon other facts that become know and outcomes of various motions that may better define the amount of recovery that is possible. Therefore, it is always good to maintain some sense of the status of the risk-adjusted return to assist with making a decision concerning whether other options, as further presented in this chapter, should be considered instead of continuing with the litigation.

License

A license is an agreement between the parties where the other party can continue to use their mark, but subject to a royalty payment of some form to the registrant. It may be deemed more cost effective to engage the alleged infringer in a license agreement ensuring the necessary provisions are in place to prevent confusion with respect to the continued use of the mark and to compromise, in some circumstances, the reputation of the registrant and their brand. As long as the license agreement includes the provisions identified below, this approach is acceptable in accommodating the registrant's requirement to police and prevent the unauthorized rampant use of the trademark.

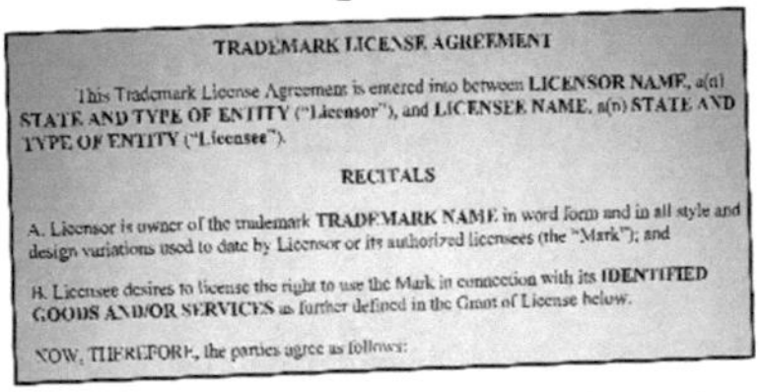

TRADEMARK LICENSE AGREEMENT

This Trademark License Agreement is entered into between **LICENSOR NAME**, a(n) **STATE AND TYPE OF ENTITY** ("**Licensor**"), and **LICENSEE NAME**, a(n) **STATE AND TYPE OF ENTITY** ("**Licensee**").

RECITALS

A. Licensor is owner of the trademark **TRADEMARK NAME** in word form and in all style and design variations used to date by Licensor or its authorized licensees (the "Mark"); and

B. Licensee desires to license the right to use the Mark in connection with its **IDENTIFIED GOODS AND/OR SERVICES** as further defined in the Grant of License below.

NOW, THEREFORE, the parties agree as follows:

To allow it to withstand scrutiny in a court, the license agreement must include quality control provisions to ensure the licensee's products bearing the mark are equal in quality to the licensor's products. Allowing the licensee to deviate in quality would be deceptive to the public. So, the registrant must continue to maintain control of the nature and the quality of the goods or services with which the trademark is associated. It is the duty of the licensor to ensure the quality control provisions are maintained to prevent loss in their right to the trademark. Pursuant to the terms of the license agreement, it is the licensee's obligation to follow the direction of the licensor with respect to these quality provisions.

If the licensee desires to apply the trademark to a new product or service, then the registrant must work to expand the description of the goods or services to include that product or service if they are in a class already registered, or enter an application to register the mark for a new class. Registration of the mark may even need to undergo territorial expansion if the licensee desires to enter a country or jurisdiction where the mark is not currently registered.

The terms of the license agreement should also provide a provision indicating that the parties will work to avoid a likelihood of confusion, and, in the event a likelihood of confusion does arise, the parties will remediate the situation causing such confusion. The license should also include provisions to accommodate the licensee in the event the licensor undergoes a merger and acquisition, goes into bankruptcy or desires to discontinue the registration of the mark. Such provisions may include the current registrant maintaining ownership of that mark, selling the mark to another that is still obligated to the provisions of the agreement, or an offer to sell the trademark to the licensee. The agreement may provide that these options are offered on some priority bases.

License agreements are also beneficial in the case of a joint venture where two parties join and decide to use the mark associated with the brand to associate with the newly developed goods or services. Adding one or more licensees according to the provisions as provided here may also help to build the identify of the brand that is associated with the mark.

The royalty rate for the license is typically based upon a valuation of the trademark at issue. Similar to other properties, trademarks may be valued according to one of three methods—(1) cost method, (2) income method and (3) marketing method.

Key provisions of the license agreement include the following:

- Title of agreement that may be expanded beyond merely Trademark License Agreement to extend to other provisions being addressed in the agreement.
- Identification of the parties.
- Effective date of the agreement.

- Recitals identifying the history of the parties and generally describing the purpose of the agreement.
- Definitions for key terms used within the agreement.
- Definition of confidential information and confidentiality provisions.
- Rights granted pursuant to the agreement (*e.g.*, exclusivity or non-exclusivity of use, etc.).
- Rights reserved by the licensor.
- Territory, which could be "whole world" or limited to certain countries and/or jurisdictions.
- Term or duration of license and termination provisions, if any, by licensor or licensee.
- Quality control provisions.
- Requirements for marking trademarks.
- Payment and/or royalties with a royalty typically being defined based upon a base rate—*e.g.*, gross sales of associated good or service.
- Reporting, payment and auditing of royalties.
- Breach of agreement provisions.
- Provisions accommodating infringement against licensor or licensee or infringement of the trademark by a third party.
- Non-compete provisions both during the term of the agreement and following termination of the agreement.
- Accommodations for changes in trademark rights, for example, expansion of scope of goods or services through description of goods or services in existing classes or the addition of new classes.
- Representations and warranties provided by licensor.
- Assignment provisions and rights of licensee to continue to use the mark in the event of a change of licensor or ownership by the licensor and maintenance of trademark rights provisions.
- Other boiler plate contract provisions.

Coexistence Agreement

A coexistence agreement is an agreement between the parties to allow each other's use of the mark to coexist allowing each party's use in selected markets and perhaps under certain other separate limitations. It is another solution for avoiding the protracted costs of litigation in the event both parties believe they can mutually agree upon a solution to use the trademark.

Typically, a need for the coexistence agreement arises due to other extenuating factors including, for example, the following:

- Clearance search identifies conflicting use.
- USPTO's refusal to accept registration of a junior mark based upon likelihood of confusion with senior, registered mark.
- Other USPTO actions including an opposition or a petition to cancel.
- Litigation
- Geographically remote user chooses to expand use into another's geographic region.
- Expansion of product or services.
- Mergers and acquisitions resulting in addition of product or service line.

The coexistence agreement provides a way for parties to continue the use of their marks, but with certain limitations.

Terms of the coexistence agreement may be included to limit a party's future registration of the mark or not allow it at all. Other provisions may be included to prevent a party from continuing with or commencing an opposition or a petition for cancellation of the mark.

The main purpose of the coexistence agreement is to define the rights that exist between the two competing mark holders, but there is also the purpose or, in the perspective of the

USPTO, the requirement of avoiding confusion among consumers over the use of the two marks. Thus, the coexistence agreement must be drafted to avoid likelihood of confusion between the two similar trademarks. There are various methods for doing this including the following with respect to the use of the marks:

- Geographical limitations;
- Trade channel limitations (*e.g.*, online, catalog, wholesalers, etc.)
- Limitations on use during particular times or circumstances throughout the year;
- Limitations on use in association with certain defined products or services;
- Defined methods on the ways the marks may be displayed.

An example of a coexistence agreement that includes geographic restrictions has been included in this chapter.

Consent Agreement

The consent agreement may arise as a result of a coexistence agreement or some other mutual agreement between the parties. The consent agreement may be submitted to the USPTO in an effort to allow for the registration of a junior mark that has been rejected based upon likelihood of confusion of the senior, registered mark.

While many foreign trademark offices merely allow a letter of consent for the trademark owner to authorize the conflicting mark to ultimately be registered, this is an extremely reduced form over the consent agreement, which is otherwise mandated in the USPTO.

COEXISTENCE AGREEMENT

This Coexistence Agreement (hereinafter "Agreement"), entered into and effective as of the _____ day of _________, 2019 (hereinafter "Effective Date"), is between Name of Senior Party (hereinafter "SENIOR PARTY"), a corporation organized and existing under the laws of the State of ____________, having a principal place of business at ________________________; and Name of Junior Party (hereinafter "JUNIOR PARTY"), a company organized and existing under the laws of the State of North Carolina having a principal place of business at 1709 S 16th St A, Wilmington, North Carolina 28401. Individually, SENIOR PARTY and JUNIOR PARTY may be referred to herein as a "Party" and, collectively, as the "Parties".

WHEREAS, SENIOR PARTY is the owner U.S. Trademark Registration No. __________ for the _____ Trademark ___________________ registered on the Principal or Supplemental Register of the United States Patent and Trademark Office (hereinafter "USPTO") and used in association with _________________ in International Class(es) ________ (hereinafter "the Registered Mark(s)");

WHEREAS, SENIOR PARTY filed its application for registration of the Registered Mark on the Principal Register of the USPTO on __________, where first use of the mark anywhere was stated to be __________, and first use of the mark in commerce was stated to be __________;

WHEREAS, JUNIOR PARTY uses and has continuously used since its incorporation on __________, the _____ mark ___________________ in association with its business that provides _________________;

WHEREAS, on __________, counsel for SENIOR PARTY sent a cease and desist letter to JUNIOR PARTY alleging JUNIOR PARTY's use of the Registered Mark "created confusion and uncertainty" and has "interfered with [SENIOR PARTY]'s business and have otherwise damage and continued to damage its reputation and goodwill";

WHEREAS, JUNIOR PARTY can demonstrate actual use of the Registered Mark in the State of North Carolina in association with _________________ at a time that predates SENIOR PARTY's first use of the Registered Mark;

WHEREAS, counsel for JUNIOR PARTY responded to the cease and desist letter of __________, on __________, indicating that JUNIOR PARTY's "common law rights to '___________________' pre-existed before any rights [SENIOR PARTY] accrued in the mark";

WHEREAS, the costs to the Parties in prosecuting and defending against the claims that could be asserted in a civil action and the potential loss of rights are anticipated to be significant both in terms of legal fees and diversion from other business pursuits;

WHEREAS, the Parties desire to put an end to any controversy, terminate any further action pursuant to the terms and conditions set forth below, settle and resolve all disputes between them and terminate, extinguish, and release all claims or causes of action against each other relating to the Registered Mark and to peacefully coexist in the use of the mark in their respective territories; and

WHEREAS, the Parties do not believe confusion is likely to result from concurrent use of their respective marks for their respective goods and services, *inter alia*, because use in accordance with this Agreement will cause any such confusion to be abated.

NOW, THEREFORE, in consideration of the mutual promises, warranties and covenants contained herein and other good and valuable consideration, the receipt and sufficiency of which is hereby acknowledged, the Parties agree as follows:

1. **Recitals.** The Parties agree that the above Recitals are true and correct and are hereby incorporated into this Agreement.

2. **<u>Acknowledgement of Rights</u>.** JUNIOR PARTY acknowledges SENIOR PARTY's ownership of and exclusive right to use the Registered Mark in connection with __________________ of International Class(es) ________ in the Senior Party's Geographic Area.

SENIOR PARTY acknowledges JUNIOR PARTY's ownership of and exclusive right to use the Registered Mark in connection with __________________ of International Class(es) ________ in the Junior Party's Geographic Area.

SENIOR PARTY and JUNIOR PARTY acknowledge that certain promotional and advertising within their respective jurisdictions may unintentionally be disseminated to the other party's jurisdiction, which will be acceptable as long as the responsible party causing the unintentional dissemination has taken reasonable precautions to prevent such dissemination.

3. **<u>Limitations on Rights</u>.** JUNIOR PARTY agrees that it will not in the future apply for registration of any service mark, trademark and/or trade name consisting of or incorporating the Registered Mark, or any term that may be confusingly similar to the Registered Mark covering such goods or related services in connection with _________________. This Agreement shall not limit the right of either party to employ the use of the term in identifying, promoting or marketing its business in their respective geographic region.

SENIOR PARTY agrees that it will not in the future attempt to expand the registration of the Registered Mark on the principal register of the USPTO.

4. **<u>Mitigation of Likelihood of Confusion</u>.** The Parties agree to take reasonable measures under the circumstances to market and promote their respective goods and associated services in such a way as to mitigate any likelihood of confusion between them, and in the unlikely event that confusion occurs, the Parties agree to notify each other of the confusion in writing, and to take adequate measures to prevent the likelihood of further confusion.

5. **<u>Cooperation in Executing Other Documents and Agreements</u>.** The Parties agree to sign such further documents and agreements as may be consistent with and reasonably necessary to affect the intent of this Agreement.

6. **<u>Mutual Releases</u>.** SENIOR PARTY, on behalf of itself and its parents, subsidiaries, divisions, present and former officers, directors, employees, agents, attorneys and controlling persons, successors, licensees, assignees, and other present or future parties in interest, expressly releases JUNIOR PARTY, and any of its subsidiaries, divisions, present and former officers, directors, employees, agents, attorneys and controlling persons, from any and all claims, demands, costs, expenses, liabilities, damages, actions, and causes of action, known or unknown, which relate to the Registered Mark, which could have been brought in a Civil Action or in any counterclaims or affirmative defenses thereto.

JUNIOR PARTY, on behalf of itself and its parents, subsidiaries, divisions, present and former officers, directors, employees, agents, attorneys and controlling persons, successors, licensees, assignees, and other present or future parties in interest, expressly releases SENIOR PARTY, and any of its subsidiaries, divisions, present and former officers, directors, employees, agents, attorneys and controlling persons, from any and all claims, demands, costs, expenses, liabilities, damages, actions, and causes of action, known or unknown, which relate to the Registered Mark, which could have been, brought in a Civil Action or in any counterclaims or affirmative defenses thereto.

7. **<u>Injunctive Relief</u>.** The Parties acknowledge and agree that any breach of this Agreement by a breaching Party may result in irreparable harm to the non-breaching Party. Accordingly, the Parties agree that if either Party breaches any section of this

Agreement, the non-breaching Party may be entitled, in addition to other remedies available to it, to an injunction to be issued by the United States District Court in the respective Division where the non-breaching Party has a principle place of business restraining the breaching Party from committing or continuing any breach of this Agreement, without the need for posting any bond or any other undertaking and without opposition by the breaching Party to such remedies or relief.

8. **Geographic Scope.** This Agreement shall be effective worldwide in all jurisdictions where the Parties' marks confront each other through use, application, or registration now or in the future.

9. **Modification of Agreement.** This Agreement encompasses the entire agreement and understanding between the parties hereto and supersedes any and all prior understandings or agreements, whether written or oral. This Agreement (including this paragraph) may not be altered, amended, modified, or otherwise changed except by a writing duly signed by all Parties hereto.

10. **Voluntary Agreement.** The Parties acknowledge that they are entering into this Agreement freely and voluntarily, that they have ascertained and weighed all the facts and circumstances likely to influence their judgment herein, that they have given due consideration to the provisions contained herein, and that they thoroughly understand and consent to all provisions hereto. Each party has reviewed this Agreement and, accordingly, the rule of construction to the effect that any ambiguities are to be resolved against the drafting party will not be employed in any interpretation of this Agreement.

11. **Severability.** If any one or more clauses of this Agreement should be later held invalid or unenforceable, the validity of the remaining clauses shall not be affected, and the Parties shall replace by mutual agreement any such clause held invalid or unenforceable.

12. **Counterparts.** This Agreement may be executed in multiple counterparts including electronically scanned copies of an executed Agreement, which taken together shall constitute one and the same instrument.

13. **Notices.** All communications required or permitted to be made under this Agreement shall be in writing and either shall be delivered personally or sent by United States Postal Service certified or registered mail, postage prepaid and return receipt requested, to the address or addresses set forth below, or to such other address or addresses as either party may notify the other pursuant to this Section. Any such communication shall be deemed to be properly given (i) if delivered personally, upon written acknowledgment of receipt after delivery to the address specified; or (ii) if posted, the earlier of the actual date of delivery, as set forth in the return receipt, or three (3) business days from the date posted pursuant to the foregoing. The addresses for the parties are as follows:

To Name of Senior Party:	To Name of Junior Party:
____________________	____________________
ATTN:_______________	ATTN:_______________
____________________	____________________
____________________	____________________

14. **Warranty of Authority**. The parties to this Agreement represent and warrant that they have the right and authority to execute this Agreement and that they have not sold, assigned, transferred, conveyed, or otherwise disposed of any interest, right, claim or demand, or portion thereof, relating to any matter in this Agreement.

The consent agreement in essence is a consent for a party to proceed with registration of their potentially conflicting mark inherently including a right to use the mark. While the rights of the consent agreement are typically not as extensive as those found in the coexistence agreement, sometimes the conflicting interests of the parties eventually arise requiring a coexistence agreement.

Rights under the consent agreement are just in association with the mark being registered for the identified international class(es) and associated products and/or services. The consent agreement still must include provisions that the parties agree to mitigate any likelihood of confusion between the use of the mark subject to registration and the registered trademark, and to take adequate measures to prevent likelihood of confusion in the event it does arise.

While a consent agreement is typically quicker to execute in order to meet the time demands of the USPTO, a coexistence agreement may be required if the parties are deemed to be competitors, other issues are envisioned to arise in the future that need to be accommodated, continued concerns over the use of the junior mark and either party's refusal to consent.

Additionally, the more information that is included in the consent agreement concerning why the parties believe confusion will be unlikely, and the more evidentiary support for these conclusions in the facts of the prosecution record or in the way of undertakings by the parties, the more that it can be assumed that the consent is based on a reasoned assessment of the marketplace, and, consequently, the more the weight the consent will be given by the USPTO.[1]

The agreement of the party to differing channels of trade is typically important to the USPTO and the parties as well. The parties prefer not to be pushing their brands to the same potential purchasers. Party interaction will still likely be necessary given, for example, potential for product expansion, third party infringement, variations in registered marks.

---

[1] *In re Donnay Int'l, S.A.*, 31 USPQ2d 1553, 1556 (TTAB 1884).

Even with a consent agreement, there is still a possibility that the examining attorney will refuse to allow registration of the mark to proceed.

Transfer of Ownership/Sale of Brand or Business

Assignment of the trademark attaches to the goodwill of the brand within the business. The transfer of goodwill of the business ensures customers are protected from deception and goodwill. There must be evidence to show that the purchasing party has obtained what is needed to carry on the business including, for example:

- Tangible assets needed to carry on with production of the goods;
- Substantial similarity of the finished goods; and
- Business status of the assignor after the transfer.

Index

Made in the USA
Las Vegas, NV
03 November 2026

57425254R00098